THE PHANTOM
OF THE POLES

BY WILLIAM REED

1906
WALTER S. ROCKEY COMPANY
NEW YORK

This Volume is Dedicated to
MY GRANDSON
SYDNEY REED SMITH

152733

CONTENTS.

ILLUSTRATIONS.

E. K. KANE.

† R. E. PEARY.

* A. W. GREELY.

SIR JOHN FRANKLIN.

G. W. MELVILLE.

‡ F. NANSEN.

C. F. HALL.

SOME FAMOUS POLAR EXPLORERS.

* From "Three Years of Arctic Service," courtesy Charles Scribner's Sons.
† From "Northward," F. A. Stokes Co. Copyright 1902 by Rockwood, N. Y.
‡ From "Farthest North." Copyright 1897 by Harper & Brothers.

U of M

INTRODUCTION.

THIS volume is not written to entertain those who read for amusement, but to establish and prove, so far as proof can be established and proved, a half-score or more of mighty truths hitherto not comprehended. This may seem boastful; but, when understood, I hope it will not be so considered; for one key will unlock them all. Throw away the key, or refuse to use it, and the truths will remain securely locked in the archives of the unknowable, as they have been since man inhabited the earth. I fully realize that the task is herculean; but as Hercules performed his tasks, I hope to do likewise. I am aware that I also have one powerful giant to tackle; but the stone in my sling may land at the place at which it is aimed, and the giant Prejudice be laid low and be succeeded by that young stalwart, General Investigation.

The problems to be solved are as follows:

1. Why is the earth flattened at the poles?
2. Why have the poles never been reached?
3. Why is the sun invisible so long in winter near the farthest points north or south?
4. What is the Aurora Borealis?
5. Where are icebergs formed, and how?
6. What produces a tidal wave?
7. Why do meteors fall more frequently near the poles, and whence do they come?
8. What causes the great ice-pressure in the Arctic Ocean during still tide and calm weather?
9. Why is there colored snow in the Arctic region?
10. Why is it warmer near the poles than six hundred to one thousand miles away from them?
11. Why is ice in the Arctic Ocean frequently filled with rock, gravel, sand, etc.?

12. Does the compass refuse to work near
the poles?

Should I be able to give reasonable
answers to the above questions—replies
that will satisfy any intelligent person—
the public will admit, I believe, that I have
fulfilled my task. Above all, I hope to be
exonerated from trying to make others believe things in which I place no credence.
So sure am I that my solutions of the
problems given above are correct, I am
willing to stake my all on their correctness.
To me, the solutions given in this volume
are perfectly clear. I have thought over
every possible objection, and all statements
are presented with certainty.

They will be taken up under separate
heads, and, thus, furnish the reader with
what the lawyers would term a brief, giving authorities on whose statements I base
my opinion. The judges, in this case, will
be the public, whom I hope to have on my
side.

Before I do this I wish to acknowledge
my indebtedness to the brave men who
have spent their time, comfort, and, many,

their lives, that all might know the truth and the geography of this wonderful world. Through their reports I am able to prove my theory that this earth is not only hollow, or double, but suitable in its interior to sustain man with as little discomfort—after getting acclimated and accustomed to the different conditions—as on its exterior, and can be made accessible to mankind with one-fourth the outlay of treasure, time, and life that it cost to build the subway in New York City. The number of people that can find comfortable homes (if it be not already occupied) will be billions.

Some have said: "Isn't it wonderful, if true?"

I am like the stranger that visited the Falls of Niagara with a friend. As he stood gazing at the falling waters, the friend remarked: "Isn't it wonderful?" "What's wonderful?" asked the stranger. "Why, the water pitching over like that." "Why," said the stranger, "I don't see anything to hinder it."

That expresses the whole situation. It

may be surprising, and seem wonderful to many, or ridiculous to others, but I see nothing to hinder it.

GENERAL SUMMARY.

To conclude that an opinion is worthless because it is not expressed in the best form is a great mistake. To study out a problem, and to be able to convey the thought clearly and forcibly to the public, is quite another thing. Whether I can state my views on this subject in a manner that will convince others, I know not; I only hope that the reader will give credit to my ideas, rather than my expression.

I claim that the earth is not only hollow, but that all, or nearly all, of the explorers have spent much of their time past the turning-point, and have had a look into the interior of the earth. When Lieutenant Greely was beholding the mock sun at 120 deg. L., he was looking into our sister-world; and when Nansen saw the square sun lined with horizontal bars, he was gazing on what may be the future home of his daughter, then but two years old.

To present these facts to the reader in order, and in a clear, concise form, let us see whether there be anything that conflicts with the claim that the earth is hollow.

1. Why is the earth flattened at the poles? As the earth is hollow, it could not be round, is the answer to that. Again, the opening to the interior would detract from its roundness just in proportion to the size of the opening.

2. Why have the poles never been reached? No poles exist, in the sense usually understood. The term, "the poles," will be used throughout this work, however, for convenience' sake, as covering the farthest point from the equator so long sought for by divers explorers.

3. Why does the sun not appear for so long a time in winter near the supposed poles? Because during the winter the sun strikes the earth obliquely near the poles. Upon the way round the curve, approaching the interior, the earth being hollow, one sinks a long way in; hence the sun shines over him; it does not show up again until it strikes that part of the earth more squarely and shines down into the basin.

4. Assuming that the earth is hollow, the interior should be warmer. We will produce what evidence we can to show that it is warmer. The ones that have explored the farthest will be the best judges.

5. We must now resort to the compass. Does it refuse to work when drawing near the supposed poles?

6. Meteors are constantly falling near the supposed poles. Why? If the earth be solid, no one can answer this question; if hollow, it is easily answered. Some volcano is in eruption in the interior of the earth, and from it rocks are thrown into the air.

7. The next query is concerning the great quantities of dust constantly found in the Arctic Ocean. What causes this dust? The volcanic eruptions that send up the rocks called shooting stars. One does not ask what this dust is composed of; for it has been analyzed, and found to be carbon and iron, supposed to come out of some volcano.

8. What produces the Aurora Borealis? The Aurora Borealis is the reflection of a

fire within the interior of the earth. The exploding and igniting of a burning volcano, containing all kinds of minerals, oils, and so on, causes much coloring; while absence of coloring, or only a faint toning, is due to the burning of vegetable matter, such as prairie or forest fires.

9. Icebergs are next in order. Where are they formed? And how? In the interior of the earth, where it is warm, by streams or canyons flowing to the Arctic Circle, where it is very cold, the mouth of the stream freezing and the water, continuing to pass over it, freezing as it flows. This prevails for months, until, owing to the warm weather in summer, the warmth from the earth, and the warm rains passing down to the sea, the bergs are thawed loose and washed into the ocean. Icebergs cannot be formed on earth, for the reason that it is colder inland than at the mouth of a stream; hence the mouth would be the last to freeze and the first to thaw. Under those conditions, icebergs could not be formed.

10. What causes tidal waves? Many

are started by icebergs leaving the place
where they were formed, and plunging into
the ocean. This answer is given because
nothing else can produce one hundredth
part of the commotion of a monster iceberg
when it plunges into the ocean. What is
the natural conclusion if an iceberg creates
the greatest commotion?   It will start the
largest waves, and send them the farthest.
Some advance the theory that the moon
starts tidal waves and keeps them going;
but it is hard to believe, as they would
have to travel more than one thousand
miles an hour, which is too fast for a wave
of water.

11. What causes colored snow in the
Arctic region?   Two causes: The red,
green, and yellow are caused by a vegetable matter permeating the air with such
density that when it falls with the snow it
colors it.   This vegetable matter is supposed to be the blossom or pollen of a plant.
As it does not grow on earth, one can
naturally believe that it must grow in the
interior.   Black snow is caused by a black
dust, consisting of carbon and iron, and

supposed to come from a burning volcano. As no burning volcano is near the Arctic Ocean, it also must come from the interior of the earth.

12. Why are the nights so long in the polar regions? In winter, the sun strikes the earth obliquely in that locality, and in approaching the supposed poles one passes down into a hollow, thus shutting out the sun until it strikes the earth more squarely.

13. What causes the great ice-pressure in the Arctic Ocean during still tide and calm weather? One of the great annoy- ances, as well as dangers, met with in the Arctic regions, is the ice-pressure. This is caused by different conditions. Refer- ence is not made to hummock or loose ice, that grinds against shore; or fast ice; but to the ice that ships get fast in and drift with. Ice-pressure arises from change of current caused by the tide setting in or out, a strong wind with a sudden change, and in calm weather, the tidal wave, most annoying of all; for it comes when not looked for, and turns everything topsy- turvy. The ice, accordingly, has no show

and must break.   A wind is different.
The whole moves along like a monster
raft.   The sea is covered, and cannot rise,
while the wind blows a perfect gale.   This,
when under cover in ship or hut, is but
little felt; but when a tidal wave puts in
an appearance, things are different.   The
wave is in motion long before it reaches
the ice-field, and the force that keeps it
moving is not interfered with by the ice,
which is lighter than the wave, else it
would sink.   When the ice, therefore, is
raised, it must break, split, and roar; but
the wave goes on.

14. Why is the ice filled with rock,
gravel, and sand?   These substances
came from an exploding volcano near
where the iceberg was formed.   As they
fall during all seasons of the year, they
appear, of course, in all stages, from the
time the stream first froze over until the
iceberg passed into the ocean.

GLOBE SHOWING SECTION OF THE
EARTH'S INTERIOR

The earth is hollow. The poles so long
sought are but phantoms. There are openings
at the northern and southern extremities. In
the interior are vast continents, oceans, mountains and rivers. Vegetable and animal life
are evident in this new world, and it is probably
peopled by races yet unknown to the dwellers
upon the earth's exterior.

THE AUTHOR.

THE PHANTOM
OF THE POLES

CHAPTER I.

FLATTENING OF THE EARTH AT THE POLES.

W HY is the earth flat at the poles? Our school-books teach that the earth is round, and flattened at the poles; but they do not tell us why. If the earth is solid, this question cannot be answered. If the earth be hollow, the question is easily answered, as it could not be hollow and at the same time round; for the opening to the interior of the earth would then detract from the roundness just in proportion to the size of the opening. A ball cannot be made round and have a hole in it: however small the hole, the ball is not round to that extent.

If the earth be double, or hollow, it is built just as it would have to be. If the earth be round, there would be no need of

this book; for that alone would settle the
question for all time.   To prove a fact,
one or two circumstances will sometimes
be sufficient; but not always.   For in-

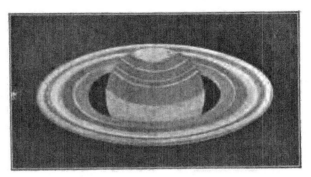

PLANET SATURN.

The planet Saturn is a world within a world, and
maybe more.   The inner world is flattened at the
poles, and is 75,000 miles in diameter.   If hollow, the
earth could move round in it, and yet not be within
20,000 miles of its walls.

stance, if it were claimed that the earth
had an opening to the interior, and one
could show that the earth was round, that
alone would be sufficient to refute it.   But,
on the other hand, the fact that the earth
is flattened at the poles is not sufficient to
prove that it is hollow, and is only one of

the evidences to show that, if it be, the earth is in the right shape for it. If now we can produce enough other evidence to prove that the earth is double, then we have shown why it is flattened at the poles. The fact that the earth is flattened at the poles is not any proof that the earth is double, or hollow. It only shows that the shape of the earth is not only favorable to such a condition, but absolutely necessary, and gives a good foundation with which to start.

CHAPTER II.

LENGTH OF POLAR NIGHTS.

If the earth be hollow—and I contend it is—that fact accounts for the sun not being visible for so long a time near the pole. As the sun strikes the earth obliquely near the poles in winter, only a slight depression would be required to shut it out entirely during the winter months; shut out until it got high enough to shine on that part of the earth more directly, or, as would be termed in more southern latitudes, higher in the skies. The farther one advanced into the interior, the longer would be the night. Were the earth solid and round, I am of the opinion that the sun could be seen nearly, if not quite, every day in the year. When Nansen saw what he called the mirage of the sun, and took it for the real sun—several days too soon for its appearance—he was much disappointed, as the *Fram* must have drifted south considerably since he took his last

Home life in the Arctic Circle.

observation. If a few days' drifting could
make such a difference in the sun's arrival,
would not the traversing of several thousands of miles be a cause for shutting out
the sun for several months? It has been
supposed, heretofore, that the farther north
one got, the longer would be the night.
That is true, in one sense; for, in going
into the interior, travelers must go north
until they reach the farthest point; but
long before they do they will have sunk a
long way into the earth, or from where
they would have been had they traveled
the same distance if the earth were solid
and round. For example: if you are
living in a valley, the sun rises later and
sets earlier than on a mountain: the entrance to the earth can be represented as a
deep valley, and the farther one advances
the deeper it becomes.

Let us propound this problem in another
shape. The supposed location of the
North Pole is from 450 to 500 miles in the
air; not straight up, but on the same angle
as going straight north from 60 degs. latitude, allowing for the natural curve of the

earth.   If one could be located there in a
balloon, one would see the sun, perhaps,
each day in the year.

In Volume I, page 375, of Nansen's
"Farthest North," Friday, January 19,
1894, he says: "Splendid wind, with velocity of thirteen to nineteen feet per second;
we are going north at a grand rate.   The
red, glowing twilight is now so bright
about midday that if we were in more
southern latitudes we should expect to see
the sun rise bright and glorious above the
horizon in a few minutes; but we shall
have to wait a month yet for that."   The
fact is, Nansen was going into the interior
of the earth, while he was under the impression that he was going north.

CHAPTER III.

WORKING OF THE COMPASS.

IF the earth be hollow, what is expected of the compass? Anyone knowing anything about a compass knows that as soon as a ship begins to turn, the needle will tip up as far as it can. To satisfy himself, let the reader take any compass and tip it toward the south. The needle will drop as far as it can. Then tip it north, and see how quickly it will rise to the glass. at the top. If a compass will work like that in New York, why should it not do the same near the poles? As soon as the curve begins, which is probably about 55 to 60 degs. latitude, the compass will try to follow north, and, in order to do so, will rise to the glass at the top, or as far as the adjustment permits.

Greely proved that when the needle was suspended on an untwisted silken thread, it stood pointing *nearly* straight up. That was at latitude 85 degs.; at 90 degs. it would be erect. That is just what would be expected if they were nearly at the turning, or at farthest point north. On the explanation that the earth is hollow, the needle worked just as it should have, and if it worked differently, would have been wrong.

A compass, or magnetic needle, is controlled by one of the laws of the universe, and when in order works accurately. If it does not seem right, it is better to halt and see if the fault be not elsewhere. The fact that the compass does not work, as some suppose, is one of the strongest arguments in favor of the theory that the earth is hollow; for, had it pointed to the supposed north, it could well be claimed that if the earth was hollow, the needle would not have pointed as it did. What seems, therefore, to be a defective compass, turns out to be one of the powerful proofs necessary to substantiate a great truth. Man had nothing to say about making the earth: that was given to an Allwise Creator; and if, in His wisdom, it was made double, or hollow, it was for some wise purpose.

As Greely's trip was for scientific purposes, great attention was paid to every branch of it. Let us note right here the observation of the magnetic needle, and see if we can account for the unruly conduct of this little metal servant that has always proved such a faithful friend to man. If the earth be hollow, and sailing in a direction that seems to be north—but, as a matter of fact, down—while holding that course you sail round the farthest point north, you gradually pass into the interior, and your head will soon be toward the north, and your feet toward the south: this would be the exact position when a ship or individual is half-way in or around the curve. The needle would then have to point straight up. What did it do? Greely says on page 127:

"For the uninitiated it should be said that the object of these readings was to note the declination of the magnetic needle. In the greater part of the world the compass does not point to the geographical pole, and the saying, 'true as the needle to the pole,' is only an inaccurate simile. The magnetic declination of any place is the difference between the geographical pole and the quarter to which the needle actually points, and is measured in degrees to east or west. For instance, where the needle points to the true west, the declination is said to be 90 degs. W., and when pointing to the southwest, to be 135 degs. W. At Fort Conger, in 1882, the magnetic needle pointed between the west and southwest, the declination being 100 degs. 13 min. W.

"In the magnetometer a small magnet, freely suspended by a single fibre of untwisted silk, swings readily in any horizontal direction. This magnet, at Conger, was never quiet, not even on what are technically known as calm days, but swung to and fro in a restless, uneasy way, which at various times impressed me with an uncanny feeling quite foreign to my nature. As it swung to right and left, its movements were clearly outlined on a fixed, illumined, glass scale, which served

as a background, and the extreme oscilla-
tions, seen through a small telescope by the
observer, were recorded.   In the other end
of the building was placed, on a stable pier,
a dip-circle, from which the inclination or

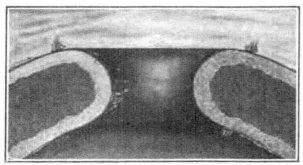

THE WORKING OF THE COMPASS.
This illustration is presented to show how the magnetic needle works in passing into the interior of the
earth, and how the compass would lead explorers out
again, they not knowing the earth was hollow.

dip of the magnetic needle was hourly
determined.   A magnetic needle, nicely
and delicately balanced, in the middle latitudes assumes a nearly level position.   At
Conger, however, the needle, adjusted so
that it can move freely in a vertical plane,

shows a strong tendency to assume an upright position.   At a dip of 90 degs. the
needle would be erect, while at Conger the
inclination was about 85 degs."

What made that needle so restless? so
much so that it caused Greely such unpleas-
ant emotions?   If that needle was suspended in the middle latitudes it would, as he
said, assume nearly a level position.   Let
us see why it takes that position, and perhaps we can then tell why it assumes a
different position when nearing the poles.
It takes the level position because gravity
draws it down, and the magnet swings it
round: there are no conflicting laws; both
act in harmony.   When one is entering
the curve to the interior of the earth, gravity draws the needle down, while the magnet pulls it up, forcing a constant conflict;
the needle must be true to the north, while
gravity is pulling down, or south.   The
result is a restless needle.   As soon as
gravity shows the stronger, the needle
must fall; but when the magnet is strong
enough to overcome gravity, the needle is
pulled in a perpendicular position, or point,

to the north. One of Nature's own witnesses here proves our case—a witness too strong to be impeached. If the needle at Fort Conger had worked, as all supposed it should have done, the defense in this case could have come into court, and shown by this witness—Mr. Compass—that the earth could not be hollow, or the needle would not have pointed as it did. Accordingly, what was regarded as a strange phenomenon, or a balky compass, turns out to be one of our best witnesses for establishing the great fact that the earth is hollow. Happily, a number of equally strong witnesses could be spared yet enough remain to prove our case.

If the earth be hollow, and the ship or needle is half-way in the interior, the little needle is still "true to Poll," and if it could speak would have said: "My friend, do not judge me so harshly: I am loyal to you, and I would gladly show you where the north is, but you hold me down, so I can't. When you suspended me on a silken thread, you gave me a better chance, and I then pointed straight up, or nearly

so; *for that was north,* or the opposite
was south, which pulled the other end of
the needle down."

By treating the earth as hollow, we
have the solution of all the great mysteries—such as the aurora, tidal waves,
ice-pressure, colored snow, open Arctic
Ocean, warmer south, icebergs, flatten-
ing of the earth at the poles, and why
the poles have not been found, the supernatural giving way to the natural, as it always does with understanding, and relief
comes to mind and body.

In Volume II, pages 18 and 19, Nansen
writes about the inclination of the needle.

Speaking of Johansen, his aide:

"One day—it was November 24th—he
came in to supper a little after six o'clock,
quite alarmed, and said, 'There has just
been a singular inclination of the needle
to twenty-four degs., and, remarkably
enough, its northern extremity pointed to
the east. I cannot remember ever having
heard of such an inclination.' He also
had several other inclinations of about fifteen degs. At the same time, through the

opening into his observatory he noticed that it was unusually light out of doors, and that not only the ship, but the ice in the distance, was as plainly visible as if it had been full moonlight. No aurora, however, could be discerned through the thick clouds that covered the sky. It would appear, then, that this unusual inclination was in some way connected with the Northern Lights, though it was to the east and not the west, as usual."

Nansen's location at that time would probably have put the compass on an angle of forty-five degs., if not more. Unless the needle was suspended on a thread, where it could move independently, it might assume any position but the right one. I am at a loss to know where to locate the attraction that moves the needle north—the magnet, or whatever it may be. Why should this needle be attracted north through any influence beyond what is derived from the earth itself? If it gets its attraction entirely from the influence of the earth, which it seems to me it *must*, then where does that attraction terminate?

If the earth be hollow, is the attraction
around the edge of the earth entering the
interior, or is it drawn to a centre half-way
betwixt the outer edges?   Until that can
be fully determined, it is hard to judge
how the needle should operate in passing
into the interior of the earth.

I have been asked what causes the compass to stand erect at the magnetic poles?
what influence draws it farther, or makes
it assume a perpendicular position?   The
opposite pole draws one end of the compass down, causing the other end, north or
south, as the case may be, to assume an
upright position.   The restlessness of the
needle at or near the magnetic poles is
thus accounted for, the force drawing it
one-half disappearing, and leaving the
opposite pole to do the work of both.
Hence a weak or vacillating needle.

CHAPTER IV.

AROUND THE CURVE.

In passing round the curve leading into the interior of the earth, it seems difficult for some people to understand how water can be made to stay on the edge of the earth. A question of that nature seems absurd to many; but it is not. While water is a liquid and seeks its level, yet the centre of gravity is all there is to "up" or "down," and affects everything in accordance with its weight. As water is heavy, gravity forces it to the earth. Whether gravity is something in the earth that draws, or something in the air or ether that repels, I do not know, nor do I know anyone that does. Whatever it be, it draws the water to the earth with such force that there is no danger of its being spilt. Gravity at the curve, or at the turning into the interior of the earth, acts like a large magnet. Take a magnet, bent in a circular form, and see if there be any difference inside or outside. The experiment will show the attraction to be the same on either side.

On page 396 Nansen again writes: "Taking everything into calculation, if I am to be perfectly honest, I think this is a wretched state of matters. We are now in about 80 degs. north latitude, in September we were in 79 degs.; that is, let us say, one degree for five months. If we go on at this rate we shall be at the pole in forty-five, or say fifty, months, and in ninety or one hundred months at 80 degs. north latitude on the other side of it, with probably some prospect of getting out of the ice and home in a month or two more. At best, if things go on as they are doing now we shall be home in eight years.

"A secret doubt lurked behind all the reasoning. It seemed as though the longer I defended my theory, the nearer I came to doubting it. But no; there is no getting over the evidence of that Siberian driftwood." (Page 303.)

Whenever the explorers pass into the interior of the earth, as they have been passing, they meet such different situations that all are puzzled to account for what, under other conditions, would be plain and simple. This shows that there is something going on entirely foreign to the ordinary fixed rules of the universe as man understands them; therefore no wonder they call it the strange land. Everyone that has spent considerable time in the Arctic or Antarctic circles has met with conditions unexplainable when based on the theory that the earth is round—each one easily accounted for, however, when treated on what now seems a fixed fact, that the earth is hollow.

When one reads reports from different explorers regarding such strange things happening in that country, one might almost conclude he was in a world of chance, or be as the Yankee farmer said when talking about rain. Chided for doubting the acts of Providence, said he: "Wal, sir, I guess He is good, but He's careless." If the earth were solid and such things happened, one might almost be led to say Providence *was* careless.

Greely's description, on page 265, of passing round the curve of the earth is exceedingly good and clear:

"The deep interest with which we had hitherto pursued our journey was now greatly intensified. The eye of civilized man had not seen, nor his feet trodden, the ground over which we were traveling. A strong, earnest desire to press forward at our best gait seized us all. As we neared each projecting spur of the high headlands, our eagerness to see what was beyond became so intense at times as to be painful. Each point reached, and a new landscape in sight, we found our pleasure not unalloyed, for ever in advance was yet a point which cut off a portion of the horizon and caused a certain disappointment."

If Greely and his companions were entering into the interior of the earth, they would certainly find that the earth has a greater curve near the poles than at any other place; and as they passed over or around the farthest point north, each projection reached would be followed by another which always seemed to take in a part of the horizon. This is just what they experienced.

"I am extremely puzzled," he added, "to understand how Gilman Glacier and its neighbor to the east discharge their surplus water. A well-marked line of low hills, at least two hundred feet in height, cuts them off from Lake Hazen, but I scanned with the telescope the entire range in vain, for anything looking like a break. The hills were but seven to nine miles distant, and the telescope was an excellent one. Lynn used the glass with the same result. It is evident the glaciers must discharge into the lake in some way. It is possible they feed lakes lying among the hills, and that they may be those seen by Bender." (Page 409.)

Had Greely known that the earth was hollow, that would have been easily decided; for he would have come to the conclusion that the water on the opposite side of those low hills discharged into some bay or fiord extending into the interior of the earth, and would reach Lake Hazen only when passing up from there.

CHAPTER V.

MYSTERIES OF THE POLAR REGIONS.

Besides the great mystery—that is, the finding of the pole—accounts of other mysteries or strange phenomena are met with in the published accounts of Arctic exploration, the writers laying an emphasis on their narratives all the more noteworthy since they do not pretend to solve the riddle propounded by Nature. A few instances culled from page 393 of Nansen's work will suffice for the present:

"That north wind is still persistent, sometimes with a velocity of nine or even thirteen feet, but yet we do not seem to be drifting south; we lie in 80 degs. north latitude, or even a few minutes farther north. What can be the reason of this? There is a little pressure every day just now. Curious that it should again occur at the moon's change of quarter. The moon stands high in the sky, and there is daylight now, too.

"Friday, February 16th.—Hurrah! A meridian observation to-day shows 80 deg. 1 min. north latitude, so that we have come a few minutes north since last Friday, and that in spite of constant northerly winds since Monday. There is something very singular about this. Is it, as I have thought all along from the appearance of the clouds and the haziness of the air, that there has been south wind in the south, preventing the drift of the ice that way, or have we at last come under the influence of a current? That shove we got to the south lately in the face of southerly winds was a remarkable thing, and so is our remaining where we are now in spite of the northerly ones. It would seem that new powers of some kind must be at work."

CHAPTER VI.

THE WATER-SKY: WHAT IT IS.

IN presenting the different reports on
the water-sky, or the ice-blink, it will be
well to point out that a reflection of the
earth's surface in the sky is of more importance than seems at first to be the case.
How hard it is for most people to believe
anything new or different from what they
were taught when young! The reflection
in the sky, as seen in the Arctic Circle, is
very peculiar. Something, not easily explained, causes the skies in that vicinity to
act as a mirror when the atmosphere is
in a certain condition: the surface of the
earth is reflected accurately. The entrance to the interior of the earth is undoubtedly the cause; but how or why, I
cannot tell; it is sufficient for our purposes,
however, to know that it positively does
act as a mirror.

To show that the sky reflects the conditions of the ice, water, and land would not

VIEW OF THE WATER-SKY.

The skies in the Arctic and Antarctic circles reflect the surface of the earth, water and ice, accurately. No great enterprise is undertaken without first consulting the water-sky.

be of so much importance: that fact could not be used to prove that the earth is hollow.   But to prove that the Aurora Borealis is nothing but the reflection of a burning volcano, prairie- or forest-fire in the interior of the earth, would be important. Quotations from the various authorities on Arctic exploration are cited here for the purpose of proving the correctness of my views.

Throughout Nansen's work he gives accounts of water-skies.   In Volume II, page 472, his diary states:

"Wednesday, March 25th—There is the same dark water-sky behind the promontory in the southwest, stretching thence westward almost to the extreme west. It has been there all through this mild weather, with southwesterly wind, from the very beginning of the month.   There seems to be always open water there, for no sooner is the sky overcast than the reflection of water appears in that quarter."

The object of quoting so many authorities on this subject is to show that what is termed "water-sky" is not the whim or fancy of one explorer, but a fixed fact, and one of the things that northern explorers always depend upon as being absolutely reliable: the condition of the surface in that country is reflected in the sky so accurately that anyone can understand it. The water-sky is seen whenever the skies are overcast. This fact supports the claim that the aurora is a great fire underneath, reflected in the sky, and must come from a burning volcano, prairie- or forest-fire in the interior of the earth.

Nansen also adds: "To judge by the sky, there must be a number of lanes in the south and southwest,"—a supposition that afterward proved to be correct,—and on page 233, Volume II, he continues:

"In front of us on the horizon we have a water-sky, or at any rate a reflection which is so sharply defined and remains so immovable that it must either be over water or dark land; our course just bears on it. It is a good way off, and the water it is over can hardly be of small extent; I cannot help thinking that it must be over land. May it be so! But between us, to judge by the sky, there seems to be plenty of lanes."

Nansen and his companion, Johansen, were endeavoring by the appearance of the sky to determine whether water, ice, or land was ahead. It happened to be water, as many lanes, representing openings in the ice, were reflected in the sky. They invariably depended upon the appearance of the sky to determine the condition of the water or ice on the earth ahead. And he mentions that soon after this the lanes were so numerous that they retarded their progress very much. Many times they were obliged to go miles around them, and in those directions found land and water, just as the sky indicated that they would. When flames flash through the heavens, wise men tell us that, instead of considering that there is fire on the earth, or in the interior of the earth, it is an Aurora Borealis, and supposed to be electricity.

It is strange that there is no difference of opinion about the reflection of land, water, or ice, while there is so much about

fire. Perhaps the only reason why there
is any difference of opinion as to what
causes the reflections of the aurora is that
no one happens to think of its being fire.
This error arose from the fact that no one
entertained the idea that the reflection
could arise from fire, as they knew nothing
about the earth being hollow.

Nansen proceeds to enlighten us concerning the water-sky, and imparts some
of his restless ambitions to us. In Volume
II, page 261, he says:

"Johansen, who has gone out, says the
same water-sky is to be seen in the south.
Why is it we cannot reach it? But there
it is, all the same, an alluring goal for us
to make for, even if we do not reach it very
soon. We see it again and again, looking
so blue and beautiful; for us it is the color
of hope."

The sky, extending over the entrance to
the interior of the earth, seems to act in
some way as a mirror, and reflects objects
of size on the surface of the earth plainly
and clearly. It is such a true mirror that
for hundreds of years people living there

WATER-SKY.

Here is another view showing how the surface of the
earth, water, and ice is reflected as in a mirror.

or those going there, learn to tell from what is reflected just what to expect.

Another explorer of the north. Kane, on page 152, writes that "as the surface of the glacier receded to the south, its face seemed broken with piles of earth and rock-stained rubbish, till far back in the interior it was hidden from me by the slope of a hill. Still beyond this, however, the white blink or glare of the sky above showed its continued extension."

Heretofore, I have quoted almost entirely from Arctic explorers in reference to the condition of the skies, and how the appearance of the latter determines the condition of the water and the ice. Bernacchi, who spent nearly two years in the Antarctic regions, declares that, in speaking of the Antarctic:

"Before noon the storm had passed, and we made strenuous efforts to reach some water to the east, which was indicated by a strongly marked 'water-sky' in that direction. Toward evening of the next day, we reached the open sea, being then in latitude 65 deg. 33 min. S. and longitude 165

deg. 48 min. E.   There was a swell from
the north, and the temperature of the sea
rose from 29 deg. 1 F. at the edge of the
pack to 30 deg. 8 F.   We were now in
very nearly the same position as we had
been six weeks before, and during those
six weeks we had burnt nearly one hundred tons of coal, with little result."
(Page 60.)

This assures us that the same sort of sky
is seen in the Antarctic regions as in the
Arctic.   Something causes it to act as a
mirror in both circles, and reflects the condition of the earth in the sky.

CHAPTER VII.

THE AURORA: ITS WONDERFUL VARIATIONS.

THE aurora is not, as supposed by many, an accumulation of electricity, or magnetic force, around the poles; it is nothing more nor less than the reflection upon the clouds, ice, and snow of a burning volcano, prairie-or forest-fire in the interior of the earth. This fancy coloring, seen in many cases, may be caused in different ways. First, the burning material—of kinds too numerous to mention—might produce any and all colors. Then the light shining through smoke, dust, or colored material in the air —the same that produces colored snow— would reflect different colors. As the flames shoot up, and are sucked, whirled, or blown in all directions, they may produce the fanciful movement in the sky, and be re-reflected by the peculiar atmospheric conditions in the polar regions. The slightest motion of a magic lantern will send the light quivering and shimmering in

many directions, or a searchlight, moved a
few inches, will throw the reflection of the
light many miles. All the changes in a
great fire, then, roving and burning first
one place, then another, shooting up anew,
as fresh material is reached, now dying
down, now exploding anew, must produce
a wonderful effect, as all agree that the
aurora does. Many have pictured the
aurora as representing fire seen in the sky,
and one would think that the theory that it
is electricity would be rejected by all, as it
was by many as soon as it was discovered
that in many cases when the aurora was
brightest the needle was not affected
in the least. For thousands of years the
aurora has been one of the most conspicuous mysteries to be solved. For that
reason, considerable space will be given to
the subject, mainly to show how it appeared to those nearest to it.

They surely will not be accused of drawing on the imagination, or of coloring their
statements in the least. When read in connection with the claim that the earth is
hollow, and the aurora is produced by a

burning volcano, an extensive prairie- or
forest-fire,—in the interior of the earth,—a
wholly different view of the aurora will be
entertained; especially when taken in connection with what has been known for
hundreds of years: that the surface of the
earth or ocean can be, and is, reflected in
the sky so correctly that whalers have long
depended upon the reflection to tell them
when open water, ice, or land lies ahead.
Men who embark upon dangerous pur-
suits, such as hunting the seal, walrus,
whale, and bear, never attempt to advance
unless the conditions be favorable: that
is always determined by what they see in
the skies.   If the sky acts as a mirror
wherein can be noted the conditions of the
ice, water, etc., would not a great fire, like
the aurora, be reflected equally as clear?
To call the fire an aurora, mock sun, or
any other name, does not change the fact
in the least.

Suppose a hunter, accustomed for years
to locating musk ox by the reflection in the
skies, should see a herd of reindeer some
morning in the same way.   What would

he do if he wanted a shot at them? Would he take his gun and start out to stalk them, or would he say: "What a strange phenomenon! I wonder what it is!" then wind up by calling the reflection by some other name? No; he would know what it meant. The strangest thing of all is that the explorers and writers on this subject did not know what the aurora was when they saw it.

Let us now take up the question of the Aurora Borealis, or the Aurora Polaris, as it is sometimes called. I contend that the aurora is nothing more nor less than the reflection of a burning volcano, prairie- or forest-fire, or fire of some kind, and that such is the fact will be proved by quoting from observations made by those who have spent considerable time on the verge of the Arctic and Antarctic regions.

The northern whalers, or those that seek game in that frozen country, look into the sky in order to tell whether the ice is frozen solid or whether there are openings. If the sky be a whitish gray, the surface reflected is covered with ice; if there

be patches of blue, they indicate openings
in the ice. Thus, they are able to tell the
condition of the earth many miles away.
If that can be done, and it has been proved
it can, why cannot we, when we see what
appears to be a fire burning in the sky,
know that there must be a fire beneath?
No reasonable person can doubt that the
same reflection is as true in one case as it is
in another. In Bernacchi's story of his
Antarctic exploration, one reads: "Owing
to the great reflection in those latitudes,
flames appeared to dart across the horizon,
and resembled a mighty conflagration.
Higher and higher they rose, changing
the color from dark red to every variety of
shade."

You note that he describes them as
"flames that appeared to dart across the
horizon, and resembled a mighty conflagration." That was just what it was.
People visiting the location nearest the
pole have experienced no great change
compared with any other part of the
world; the told, heat, wet, the dry, and
the air are the same. Then why should

electricity or falling stars be more prevalent there than elsewhere? There is but
one answer: the exploding volcano produces both.

On page 92, Bernacchi writes: "At nine
o'clock in the evening of the 15th of March
we witnessed our first Aurora Polaris during clear, calm weather, the temperature
at the time being sixteen degrees Fahr.
The light first emanated in a waving curtain from the southeast and went round
to the southwest. The motion of the
arrow-like beams, constituting the curtain,
was rapid and at times would run along
with an undulating motion, then suddenly
shoot downward toward the earth. Seen
for the first time, it was a wondrous sight,
and to me appeared *like some great searchlight directed towards the earth from the
depths of infinity*" (the italics the one who
quotes). What could more convince one
that there is a volcano burning in the interior of the earth? He adds: "This
further display was very poor compared
with some subsequently witnessed."

Here we have another great proof that

the aurora is not electricity; for it occurs in terrible storms, storms not so terrible, and in clear, calm weather.

On page 129 Bernacchi again refers to the aurora:

"At Cape Adare (latitude 71 deg. 185) the aurora was generally observed in the north, very rarely in the south, and it always manifested itself in exactly the same manner." If it were an electric display, as has been claimed heretofore, it would be as apt to occur at one place as at another, but it always comes in the same direction and in the same form.

The author asserts, again, on page 130:

"But what was of greatest interest in the observation of the aurora was the connection which appeared to exist between it and approaching atmospheric disturbances. A strong gale from E. S. E. and S. E. was almost invariably preceded by a most brilliant and rapid auroral display. This was not a mere coincidence, but a fact repeatedly observed." What would be the natural result if a tremendous volcano had exploded? Would it not force out strong

wind?—just what he says did occur; if it
had not, there would have been great cause
for wonder.

"At 10 o'clock in the evening of June 3d
an exceedingly grand aurora was visible,"
continues Bernacchi; "it was a dazzling
and incomparable spectacle, and first manifested itself in the usual manner by a
luminous display in the north. This, however, was only a transient phase, for the
flow of streamers gradually faded away,
and the whole display lost its brilliancy
and rapidity of motion in about an hour,
leaving a glow in the sky like the *dying
embers of a great fire.*"

The italics in this quotation, like in
the one on a preceding page, are mine,
but the matter therein is but one more
instance of the general comparison of
the aurora with fire. Yet, in almost
the same breath, Bernacchi adds: "How
little we understand the nature of its
origin!" In this description he has rec-
ognized the fact that the aurora comes
usually from the same direction, and he
simply says, "in its usual manner by lumi-

nous display in the north." If he were
looking south at a fire, it naturally would
throw its reflections past him to the north.
He speaks of it "leaving a glow in the sky,
like the dying embers of a great fire."

It will be observed that this aurora
manifests itself in the *usual manner*. If
caused by electricity, is it not remarkable
that it should always come from the same
direction, and in the same form? One
would surmise that there was a mammoth
electric battery located at that place, and in
a deep well, as he describes it, *"like some
great searchlight directed towards the
earth from the depths of infinity."* The
description is right, but the conception is
wrong. What he describes was an exploding volcano in the interior of the earth
near the Antarctic entrance, and, as Poe
says, "only that, and nothing more."

We will now go to the North Pole for
other descriptions of the aurora, and see
what has been found there.

Nansen states that the aurora was
brightest in the south; just the reverse of
what Bernacchi said when he looked to-

ward the South Pole. If it was a fire, would it not have been exactly as those two men described it? To the one look-.ing south, the reflection would have been in the north; to the one looking north, the reflection would have been in the south, which was exactly the case.

I quote Nansen from another page, 394: "To-day another noteworthy thing happened, which was that about midday we saw the sun, or, to be more correct, an image of the sun, for it was only a mirage. A peculiar impression was produced by the sight of that glowing fire lit just above the outermost edge of the ice. According to the enthusiastic descriptions given by many Arctic travelers of the first appearance of this God of Life after the long winter night, the impression ought to be one of jubilant excitement; but it was not so in my case. We had not expected to see it for some days yet, so that my feeling was rather one of pain, of disappointment, that we must have drifted farther south than we thought. So it was with pleasure I soon discovered that it could not be the

sun itself. The mirage was at first a flat-
tened-out glowing red streak of fire on the '
horizon; later there were two streaks, the
one above the other, with a dark space between; and from the maintop I could see
four, or even five, such horizontal lines
directly over one another, and all of equal
length, as if one could only imagine a
square dull red sun with horizontal dark
streaks across it." Nansen imagined that
he saw the sun, but afterward claimed that
it was a mirage. What he saw was
neither. I think it was the volcano itself;
and, as he states, he saw it three days in
succession, or the two following days.
This proves that it could not have been a
mirage, inasmuch as a mirage does not
last three days. His ship had simply
drifted far enough into the interior to get
a glimpse of this volcano. You note that
he describes it as being "just at the edge
of the ice"—that is, looking toward the
north. The sun, if visible at all, would
have been in the opposite direction; it is
never square, but always round. ·He
describes what *he* saw as a square fire, ·and

afterward says he could *almost see it* assume a round form. "Both to-day and
yesterday we have seen the mirage of the
sun again; to-day it was high above the
horizon, and almost seemed to assume a
round disk-like form." (Page 398.) I
cannot imagine in what condition the fire
was or how his eyes were.

If this light was not the sun, what was
it? A fire in the interior of the earth, possibly not very far in, but, nevertheless, in
the interior. There is no reason why it
should not have been half-way or one-
third of the way in. Just when one is on
earth or in the interior is difficult to determine, as the curve is so gradual; some may
call one point the interior, while others call
a point much farther in still on earth. It
reminds one of the farmer who was asked
how old a heifer is when she becomes a
cow. He stopped to think for a moment,
then said: "I don't believe I know, as one
of my neighbors has a three-year-old cow,
and another has a four-year-old heifer."
The exact location of the dividing line will
always be a question. When the needle

points straight up it will be as near the dividing line as can be determined—near enough for all practical purposes, unless one nation should claim the earth, and another the interior. In that case, if it should appear that valuable mines are located at that point, some trouble might arise between the claimants.

In Vol. I, page 280, Hall describes "an aurora with but slight coloring. Nearly all day on the 6th, beautiful auroral displays were seen. During the morning, luminous though faint clouds were observed in different parts of the heavens. At 3 p. m., the sky being clear and the breeze light from the south, these clouds, in the form of an arch, extended from northeast to southwest, enlarging toward the northeast and accumulating above the mountains. In half an hour they resumed their original shape, and appeared in the form of light-yellow and white bands. These phenomena were present during the whole evening, being seen in every direction. Fantastic forms of light came and went rapidly, and a frequent appearance was that of a cirro-stratus cloud. On the morning of the 7th, a perfect arch extending from the north to south was observed. It consisted of uniform bands of yellow and white."

Siemens says in his journal, Hall, Vol. I, page 281, that on January 10, 1872, at five in the morning, "a bright arc was seen in the sky passing from the western horizon through the zenith to the east, parallel with the Milky Way, and distant from it about 12 degs. It disappeared about 6 a. m., leaving three clouds of similar brightness. This phenomenon, if electric, *did not show itself in the needle.*"

This, then, is another instance where the aurora does not affect the needle.

Corroborative of this, Siemens adds, "This phenomenon, if electric, did not show itself in the needle." Take either horn of the dilemma: if it was not electric, what was it? If it *was* electric, why did it not affect the needle?

Here follows a description, by Hall, page 297, of an aurora produced by a

AURORA BOREALIS.

There is nothing about this aurora, as described by Hall, that a great fire in the interior of the earth would not furnish a solution.

great volcanic eruption, very different from the account just cited. "It may be said, in general, that the greatest disturbances occurred several hours before an aurora was visible. The following short description of the display is condensed from Mauch's journal: 'At 7 p. m., as I was returning to the ship from the observatory, I noticed the slaty appearance of the sky to the northwest and the occasional shooting up of luminous streamers. At 7:15 the horizon to the northwest was a blood-red color, while faint, white streamers sprang up in rapid succession, increasing in numbers, and rising from the west, north, and northeast points. They were all directed toward the zenith, and the exterior ones bending inwards gave to the whole configuration a dome-like shape. They then all vanished, and new ones began to rise slowly from a wider extent of horizon. At 8:30 new and very bright streamers advanced toward the zenith from all directions. At 8:45 they all gathered about the zenith and formed a perfect corona. They then all seemed to move toward the north, as new ones arose from the south.' Mauch watched the progress of these streamers while passing over some stars, and assigned to them a motion of between six and seven seconds to a degree. They moved from west to east. As the corona opened and moved toward the north, a beautiful curtain was formed, its colors being very intense and bright, between yellow and white."

" 'At 3:30 p. m. I observed,' says Mauch in his journal, 'on the northeast, east, and southeast horizon, beams of luminous clouds. They soon accumulated and formed an irregular arch due east which slowly moved, as if driven, in a southerly direction. At 4 p. m. a new arch extended from nearly due east to nearly due south. At 4:10 p. m. three distinct arches, one above the other, were formed slowly in the southwest and south, exhibiting a very brilliant display, though fading very soon away. Those to the south were an intense straw-color, and formed a brilliant spectacle.' "

Can any better refutation of the theory

that the aurora is electricity be offered for the consideration of the man who thinks? Does electricity ever move through the heavens as if driven slowly along by some unseen agency? Who ever heard of electricity moving slowly, or being driven in the air?

The eruption which caused this great agitation did not ignite at once to any extent, but threw out so much dust, dirt, and smoke, that it obscured the light for several hours. As the needle was most disturbed several hours before this aurora appeared, that is evidence that the eruption of the volcano which liberated the minerals and gases, and produced the shock, was what agitated the needle, and not electricity, as hitherto supposed; for there was no aurora when the needle was most affected. When the strong coloring, shown in the aurora, did appear, it was another proof that the coloring arises from the burning of minerals, gas, oils, etc. Taken in connection with the wonderful display, the beautiful coloring and the heavy clouds, everything points to one cause—a great explosion. If this was electricity, would it have risen slowly? No; electricity is anything but *slow*. This acted as a fire, dying down, then starting up over a wider extent. It is characteristic of a fire to spread if it can find anything to consume. This aurora lasted all night, and all the next day.

Hall further asserts, on page 300: "At 5:30 p. m., on the 8th, I observed a very bright luminous arch of streamers somewhat extending from the northeastern horizon to the southwestern. When I first saw it, it was a little to the northwest of the zenith, but the whole arch seemed to move, and at 6:30, it just passed the zenith, and then had a position southeast of it, where it gradually broke up. Its southwestern extremity just touched the twilight curve, where it vanished. At 6:30 the usual haziness of the sky after the occurrence of these, was noticed."

I wish here to emphasize this point—one corroborative of my claim: "At 6:30 the usual haziness of the sky after the occurrence of these was noticed." Does electricity generally leave the sky hazy? Hall uses the words *"usual haziness"* as descriptive of the normal condition of the skies after those auroral displays.

"When above my head, it seemed less than a pistol-shot distant. Indeed, it was near by. When I moved quickly, running up to the top of the hill by the igloo, making a distance of less than 50 fathoms, the arch of the aurora, that seemed stationary while I was by the igloo and intransitive, was now several degrees to the southwest of me. I returned as quickly to the igloo, and the auroral belt was directly overhead. So small a base, with so palpable a change in bearing of the aurora, proved that it must have been quite close to the earth. A ball of fire fell during the display, and burst just before it reached the earth, throwing out prismatic scintillations in every direction." (P. 83.)

Note what he says about the wind: "A smart breeze from the north was blowing nearly the whole night. This seemed to add to the briskness of the merry dancers as they crossed the heavens to and fro." Now if this reflection was caused by electricity, would the wind have added to its briskness? I think not; but if a fire caused the reflection, then a wind would produce the effect he describes: "When over my head, it seemed less than a pistol-shot distant," he says. So small a base, with such a palpable change in the bearing of the aurora, proved that it must have been quite close to the earth.

Hall found himself unable to decide whether any noise actually came from the aurora. On asking the Innuits whether they were accustomed to hear noises during its displays, they answered, "Yes," one of them endeavoring to imitate the sound by a puffing noise from his mouth; this noise, says Hall, accorded remarkably with what he thought *he* had heard during the time of the most active display.

I have quoted extensively from Captain Hall, as he has written a very fine description of the aurora. His description will enable anyone to form an opinion as to what the aurora is—electricity or the reflection of fire.

Lieutenant Hooper, R. N., second in command of Lieutenant Pullen's boat expedition from Icy Cape to Mackenzie River, spent the winter of 1849-50 near Fort Franklin, on Bear Lake. "I have heard the aurora," wrote he in his journal, "not once, but many times; not faintly and indistinctly, but loudly and unmistakably; now from this quarter, now from that, now from one point on high, and at another time from one low down. At first it seemed to resemble the sound of field-ice, then it was like the sound of a water-mill, and at last, like the whirring of a cannon-shot heard from a short distance." Hooper admits that he heard the aurora many times, loudly and unmistakably. There can be little doubt that many people have heard the explosion, and the noise caused by the force of the fire. The light reflected in the skies could not make a noise, but its occurrence at the time of the explosion would, and as noise moves more slowly than light, it might have arrived, perhaps, when the latter was most brilliant.

"There is no satisfactory evidence," says Professor Loomis, "that the aurora ever emits an audible sound. The sound supposed to have been heard has been described as a rustling, hissing, crackling noise. But the most competent observers, who have spent several winters in the Arctic regions, where auroras are seen in their greatest brilliancy, have been convinced that this supposed rustling is a mere illusion. It is, therefore, inferred that the sounds which have been ascribed to the aurora must have been due to other causes —such as the motion of the wind, or the crackling of the snow and ice in consequence of their low temperature. If the aurora emitted any audible sound, this sound ought to follow the auroral movement after a considerable interval. Sound requires four minutes to travel a distance of fifty miles. But the observers who report noises succeeding auroral movements make no mention of any interval. It is, therefore, inferred that the sounds which have been heard during auroral exhibitions are to be ascribed to other causes than the aurora." (Treatise on Meteorology, page 186.)

The sound supposed to have been heard has been described as a rustling, hissing, crackling noise. Isn't that a pretty good description of a terrible fire at a distance? To me, it seems one of the best descriptions. Loomis further says that if the aurora emitted any audible sound, that sound ought to follow the auroral movement after a considerable interval. That would be correct if it had its origin in, or was caused by, electricity; but not if caused by the bursting of a volcano, as that would eject such an immense amount of smoke, dust, dirt, and rock that several minutes would elapse before the light or fire could shine through it; therefore the sound might reach the ear at the same time that the light reached the eye. The northern Indians give to the aurora what seems to us a curious name, *ed-thin,* that is, deer—from their having seen hairy deerskin emit sparks when briskly stroked. The southern Indians believe it to be the spirit of departed friends dancing. When it varies in color and form, they say their deceased friends are very merry.

An impressive description of the aurora is given by Nansen on page 253: "Presently the Aurora Borealis shakes over the vault of heaven its veil of glittering silver—changing now to yellow, now to green, now to red. It spreads, it contracts again, in restless change; next it breaks into waving, many-folded bands of shining silver, over which shoot billows of glittering rays, and then the glory vanishes. Presently it shimmers in *tongues of flame* over the very zenith, and then again it shoots a bright ray right up from the horizon, until the whole melts away in the moonlight, and it is as though one heard the sigh of a departing spirit. Here and there are left a few waving streamers of light, vague as a foreboding—they are the dust from the aurora's glittering cloak. But now it is growing again; new lightnings shoot up, and the endless game begins afresh. And all the time this utter stillness, impressive as the symphony of infinitude."

"Presently it shimmers in tongues of *flame* over the very zenith, and then again it shoots a bright ray right up from the horizon." He speaks of the dust: "They are the dust from the aurora's glittering cloak." When one reads that description, quoted twice from one who spent two years watching the sky for the reflection of open water, ice, or land, it passes comprehension that it did not occur to him that the aurora was nothing but the reflection of a great fire. One is reminded of Miranda in Shakespeare's "Tempest." "More to know did never meddle with my thoughts."

On another occasion, Nansen saw a remarkable display of aurora about three o'clock in the afternoon. In a lengthy description, of which I cite briefly: "On the southwestern horizon lay the glow of the sun; in front of it light clouds were swept together—like a cloud of dust rising above a distant troop of riders. Then dark streamers of gauze seemed to stretch from the dust-cloud up over the sky, as if it came from the sun, or perhaps rather as if the sun were sucking it in to itself from the

whole sky." Here we have other mention
of that ever-present and annoying dust.

In an account by Greely of a remarkable aurora (page 183) there is further
evidence of the correctness of my opinions.
"The aurora of January 21st was wonderful beyond description," he writes, "and I
have no words in which to convey any
adequate idea of the beauty and splendor
of the scene. It was a continuous change
from arch to streamers, from streamers to
patches and ribbons, and back again to
arches, which covered the entire heavens
for part of the time. It lasted for about
twenty-two hours, during which at no moment were the phenomena other than vivid
and remarkable. At one time there were
three perfect arches, which spanned the
southwestern sky from horizon to horizon.
The most striking and exact simile, perhaps, would be to liken it to a conflagration
of surrounding forests as seen at night
from a cleared or open space to their
centre. During the display Sergeant Rice
exposed a sensitive dry photographic
plate toward the aurora without any effect,

but the experiment was a doubtful one from the shifting of the light. In general, the aurora was quite colorless, though occasionally red tints were reported. Despite the remarkable duration and extent of the aurora, the magnet was but slightly disturbed. During the display the new moon appeared, a narrow crescent which, strange to say, was exactly the color of blood."

The reader will note that, despite the remarkable duration and extent of the aurora, the magnet was but slightly disturbed. This aurora was undoubtedly just what it seemed to be—a forest-fire in the interior of the earth. He does not speak of any storms or clouds such as would ordinarily accompany an exploding volcano, and, in addition, its length— twenty-two hours—makes it different from the ordinary aurora. The reader should remember this description of the aurora—a brilliant one, but almost colorless. Reddish tints were occasionally reported, but Greely saw none. This shows that the auroras that have so much color come from a burning volcano, and that the coloring is caused by the material being burned This was a prairie- or forest-fire —the same as we have on earth—and was reflected in the sky as truly as water, ice, and land. Does it not seem more reasonable that such was the case than that it was a different kind of electricity? This aurora was a plain white one, with the merest trifle of coloring, while the regular aurora has all the coloring of the rainbow. The difference is that one burned a vegetable matter, the other vegetable, mineral, oil, and everything else. Greely states that the needle was but little disturbed: a great explosion, in which large quantities of minerals, gases, and other matter are thrown into the air, might disturb the needle, but I am not sure. That would depend upon what was liberated by the explosion, and how near was the needle.

Sir George Nares remarks that, "contrary to the popular belief, the aurora gives us no appreciable light." In Greely's experience, the light was considerable on several occasions, and during the aurora, the description of which is printed above, Greely saw his shadow, at a time when a brilliant display was in one quarter of the heavens only. Tromholt says that "the very greatest amount of light which the Aurora Borealis emitted, or which, in my case, I was able to ascertain during my entire sojourn in Lapland, may be compared to that of the moon two and a half days after full, when 25 degs. above the horizon and the sky is clear."

It has been claimed that the aurora gives no light. If fire produces the aurora, it must give light.

Greely also remarks that on January 23d, print, such as is used for leading articles (termed long primer by printers), could be read with some difficulty at noon. This test, however, was not satisfactory, owing partly to the presence of the moon, but more to the remarkably varying capacity of eyes for this work. A brilliant meteor was observed in the north about 7:35 a. m., which burst into fragments, all colorless except one, which was a brilliant red. No detonation was heard.

"The Northern Lights were wonderful,"
says Nansen in Vol. II, pages 446, 447.
"However often we see this weird play of
light, we never tire of gazing at it; it seems
to cast a spell over both sight and sense till
it is impossible to tear one's self away. It
begins to dawn with a pale, yellow, spec-
tral light behind the mountain in the east,
like the reflection of a *fire far away*. It
broadens, and soon the whole of the eastern sky is *one glowing mass of fire*. Now
it fades again, and gathers in a brightly
luminous belt of mist stretching towards
the southwest, with only a few patches of
luminous haze visible here and there.
After a while scattered rays suddenly
shoot up from the fiery mist, almost reaching to the zenith; then more; they play
over the belt in a wild chase from east to
west. They seem always darting nearer
from a long, long way off. But suddenly
a perfect veil of rays showers from the
zenith out over the northern sky; they are
so fine and bright, like the finest of glittering silver threads. Is it the fire giant,
Surt himself, striking his mighty silver

harp, so that the strings tremble and sparkle in the glow of the flames of Muspellsheim? Yes, it is harp-music, wild storming in the darkness; it is the riotous war-dance of Surt's sons. Again at times it is like softly playing, gently rocking, silvery waves, on which dreams travel into unknown worlds."

Authorities too numerous to mention, —but some of them I cite—unconsciously confirm, by their vivid descriptions, that the aurora is not caused by electricity; that when it assumes any form that can be described it is likened unto a great conflagration, an exploding volcano, or the dying embers of an extensive fire, none of which in any form resembles electricity. When it cannot be described, it is more likely to be caused by the reflection and the re-reflection of the sun shining upon the ice, snow, and frost from the opposite pole.

If in the mind of the reader a doubt still exists that the aurora is not caused by electricity, the following quotations are given him to ponder:

"It seems to be the experience here that the magnet is undisturbed during the prevalence of colorless auroras, but shows marked disturbances during the vivid displays of color and sudden, violent, changes of . form."—Greely, App. 13, November 16.

" . . . an auroral display which remained continuous during the greater part of the day. It first appeared in dim patches, in the northwest about 15 deg. above the horizon, which gradually brightened and took the shape of a regular cone, which lasted for five minutes or more, while from its well-defined summit ascended luminous auroral clouds with a whorling or curling motion. These clouds emanated apparently from the summit of the cone, in the form of sharply defined, spasmodic puffs, such as are seen at times issuing from the smoke-stack of a locomotive. The clouds thus thrown out immediately diffused and disappeared without assuming any marked formation."—Greely, App. 13, November 19.

"Magnetic disturbance again occurred,

and five-minute readings were kept up from 5 p. m. Aurora appeared shortly after the disturbance of the magnet commenced."—Greely, App. 13, November 20. Extract from C. B. Henry, November 16, 1882.

"I happened yesterday, while at work outdoors, to look toward Bellot Island, and saw a small, dim, auroral light appear from azimuth about North 260 deg. East. which gradually became brighter and shot up to an altitude of about 20 deg. The best idea that I can give of its formation or movement is about like the smoke ascending and curling up from the crater of a volcano, being discharged in puffs and floating away in a luminous mass."— Greely, App. 13, November 20. Journal of D. L. Brainard, November 16, 1882.

"The only display witnessed by me was this morning, between ten and eleven o'clock. A bright streamer sprang from the southern horizon, gradually approaching the zenith with a labored movement, closely resembling the spasmodic puffs of smoke arising from a working locomotive.

Remaining in this position a short time, it was gradually dissipated and slowly dis-

AURORA BOREALIS.

The Aurora Borealis, as seen and described by D. L. Brainard, November 16, 1882, in Greely's Appendix. After observing the above engraving, read what an authority says about it; then determine its origin. Will you call it electricity? If not, what was it?

appeared."—Greely, App. 13, Journal of C. B. Henry, November 17, 1882.

"The aurora of this morning was a very low one, and we are, I think, the only party that ever could say we were in the midst of electric light.   In fact, its alarming close proximity scared one of our members considerably."—Greely, App. 13, Journal of C. B. Henry, Nov. 17, 1882.

"The light emitted during the most intense brightness was fully equal to that of a full moon, and entirely eclipsed all but stars of the first magnitude.   Objects in the landscape were plainly visible and abundant.   The height which the display maintained above the earth was at no time at a greater elevation than of cumulus clouds, and apparently almost touched the ground, but no noise of any kind was audible."—Ext. from Journal of G. W. Rice, November 17, 1882.

"Coming out of the dark quarters, all who observed it felt at first blinded; and the curtain at one time appeared so near above their heads that Gardiner and Israel speak of having unconsciously dodged to avoid it.   Israel, who is a very close and intelligent observer, thinks that at times the aurora could not have been more than one hundred feet from the earth."—From Journal of D. C. Ralston, Nov. 17, 1882.

"It appeared so low down at times that I raised my hand instinctively, expecting to bathe it in the light. The sky was entirely free from clouds, and the light of second-magnitude stars was eclipsed. The magnetic needle was violently agitated, and five-minute readings of the needle continued. The aurora visible all day long. Objects during the finest display were as plainly visible as by the light of the full moon."—Extract from Journal of H. S. Gardiner, November 17, 1882.

"The whole heavens seemed one mass of colored flames, arranged and disarranged and rearranged every instant. The display was so close to the earth that we repeatedly put up our hands as though we would touch something by so doing. There was one person who was so much affected by the display at its grandest moments that he lowered his head and put up his hands as though to ward off a blow." —From Journal of D. L. Brainard, November 17, 1882.

"In the northern sky there gradually appeared an intense vermilion color, which expanded for 10 deg. above the horizon, and remained for several minutes in this manner, its extreme brightness suggestive to the mind of a great conflagration.

"A few minutes earlier than the time which I have recorded, Gardiner witnessed a display of unusual grandeur, and of which the latter is but a slight modification. It was of unparalleled brilliancy, and its light equal to the full moon. The prismatic colors were at one time discernible. Israel and Lynn also saw it when it was at its zenith of splendor, and both speak of its near approach to the earth, and the rapidity of its movements through the heavens."

Were it not that the aurora has been the subject of thought for our greatest minds for thousands of years, so much space would not be devoted to it. Yet it is difficult to pass by without comment such descriptions of the aurora as Greely gives in his Appendix.

Electricity is never found acting like the puffings of a stationary engine, or a burning volcano, its smoke rising and slowly drifting away.

When one attempts to give the reasons why the aurora could not be the result of electricity, they multiply so rapidly and are so convincing that it seems a waste of time to give them all.

Before concluding the chapter on the aurora, I wish to assign one more probable reason why the latter is seen more frequently in the Arctic regions in the winter, and brighter than in summer. The sun shines through the earth from the southern opening through the interior of the earth. The rays of the sun strike the ice, snow, and frost, and act as a mammoth kaleidoscope, re-reflecting the sun's rays many times, and sending forth a most dazzling effect. That reflection from the sun can appear only in winter, because summer at one pole is winter at the other. It is the only season, therefore, when the sun shines directly into the opening at the South Pole, and this condition would apply only when the interior of the earth was free from clouds, as they would shut out the sun in the same

manner as on earth.   The sun's rays are
the same in the interior of the earth as on
the exterior.   One must understand that
the position of the earth is much of the
time moving with the poles or ends to the
sun.   In proof of that, there is the midnight sun at the poles, or, in other words,
during the winter the sun does not set
in the Antarctic, and during summer (the
earth having changed ends to the sun) it
does not set in the Arctic Circle.   That
gives the interior of the earth the rays of
the sun about eight months out of the
twelve.   This is another proof of the great
wisdom of the Creator, as it does away
with that long, dark winter so much
dreaded at the poles, as they have two
summers, and two short winters, to one
summer and one winter on earth.   This
does not detract in any way from the
claim that the Aurora Borealis is caused
by exploding volcanoes, prairie- or forest-
fires, but accounts for the increased frequency of the aurora in the Arctic regions
during winter.

When the reader takes into account the

wonderful variety of the aurora, and then considers the various causes which produce them, does not the above reasoning seem more reasonable than to conclude that the different kinds come from one cause—electricity?

Another reason why the aurora is brighter in the north than in the south, when produced by the sun's rays, is that the opening to the interior of the earth is much greater in the south than in the north. This is proved by the fact that the explorers have reached only within seven hundred and fifty miles of the supposed pole in the south and have passed the magnetic pole; while in the north they have been within five hundred miles of the pole, and also passed the magnetic pole, thus showing that the opening to the southern entrance to the interior of the earth is fifteen hundred miles in diameter, while it is only one thousand miles at the North Pole. That would make the sun's rays more powerful at the north than at the south. To illustrate the point, take a tin horn, and hold the big end to an electric light, then turn the little end to the light. The difference will be observed very quickly.

It will be noticed that in almost every description of the aurora, the mind naturally reverts to fire. Writers describe it in almost every form of fire. Nansen's description of it as the reflection of a great fire, is magnificent. As that is what it was, there is no need of commenting on the subject.

In submitting the question as to what produces the aurora, I merely ask that the reader use his common sense, apart from what his opinions on the matter have been. If, after reading the extracts adduced to prove the truth of my contention and my comments thereon, he still thinks the aurora electricity, let him tell why it is of such different coloring; why it always appears at the same place; why always at the poles. Electricity is universal. An electrical battery will work in one manner over all the world. Why, then, does electricity appear in the form of the aurora at the poles only? Why is the needle not always affected? Everything tends to prove that the aurora is *not* electricity. There is not a single condition, either form, color, or time, for which a fire in the interior of the earth does not furnish an intelligent solution. On the other hand, if the aurora were electricity, the coloring would be the same as the color of lightning, and as varied in location. The aurora appears by day or night, in stormy weather or in clear, wind or no wind, and sometimes it lasts ten minutes only; while at others it exists four or five days.

Does that seem like electricity, or fire?

CHAPTER VIII.

METEORS OR VOLCANIC DISTURBANCES.

Herman Siemens—who was with Captain Hall on his last trip—writes about meteors on page 257 of Hall's book: "We also saw numerous shooting stars, sometimes forming, as it were, a silver thread, from the point where they first appeared to that of disappearance; in a few instances I have seen small fireballs pushing out from them similar to those of a rocket."

I have claimed, from the start, that meteors, or so-called shooting stars, are nothing but rocks thrown up from the earth by an exploding volcano. Could so many shooting stars, as they are termed, come from a passing comet, and land near the North Pole in a bunch, when it would probably take them months, if not years, to reach the earth? Let us drop this supernatural business, and get down to common sense, and call a stone a stone, and a fire a fire. This misnaming should be done away with forever. Our children should be taught differently, and the sooner the better. The laws of the universe are absolute and immutable, and no part of a star, planet, or comet can be detached from the main body and sent sailing through space to land on this earth near the North or South Pole.

"Far in the west falls shower after shower of stars," writes Nansen in Vol. II, page 444, "some faint, scarcely visible, others bright like Roman candles, all with a message from distant worlds. Low in the south lies a bank of clouds, now and again outlined by the gleam of the Northern Lights; but over the sea the sky is dark; there is open water there."

Does anyone, able to read, believe that shower after shower of stars fall near the North Pole? If there be such a person, it is apparent that he never gave the matter any thought, or is incapable of thinking. That rocks should be called thus! If a firefly were called the sun, or a microbe an elephant, it would be no more absurd. Meteors are just plain rocks thrown out from the earth by an exploding volcano. An aurora might not always appear when these rocks fall, as an explosion might not ignite, or the burning be so small as not to show through the smoke and dust.

On the same page Nansen again writes: "Thursday, December 12th.—Between six and nine this morning there was a number of shooting stars, most of them in Serpentarius. Some came right from the Great Bear; afterwards they chiefly came from the Bull or Aldebaran, or the Pleiades. Several of them were very bright, and some drew a streak of shining dust after them."

What is more characteristic than that the shining dust should follow a volcanic eruption throwing out these shooting stars? The Great Bear is located in the right direction. My contention is that shooting stars are meteors passing through the air, thrown up by a volcanic eruption, and all meteors that have struck the earth come out of the earth, internally or externally. This theory about passing comets is given in lieu of a better one, and will not be advanced after the earth is shown to be hollow. Hall remarks that the small base of one aurora proved it to be quite close to the earth. A ball of fire fell during the display, and burst just before it reached the earth, throwing out prismatic scintillations in every direction.

Peary writes on page 163 that "a brilliant meteor was seen on the northeastern sky, descending vertically, and a little later a meteor with red and green trail was seen traveling west, about half-way to the zenith and with a slight downward angle." Those two meteors were of the many found in the vicinity of the North Pole, and undoubtedly came from a volcano in the interior of the earth.

He also noticed a peculiar phenomenon: the "apparent sinking of large areas of snow accompanied by peculiar muffled reports, which rumbled away beneath the crust in every direction until they died away."

This could be accounted for by the volcanic disturbances in the earth, from which frequent explosions send forth stone, rocks, and dust, that fall often in that part of the world..

To show that meteors are more likely to originate in the earth than from some passing comet or from other source, it should be noted that when analyzed they show no ingredients not found on earth. One writer in Clerk's Astronomy, page 389, says: "The nearest affinities of the mineral aggregated in them are with volcanic products from great depths. These meteorites seem broken-up fragments of the interior parts of globes like our own."

There is a meteor on exhibit at the Museum of Natural History, New York, weighing many tons. If that had come from some comet a few million miles away it would have struck the earth with such force that it would have penetrated the hardest rock-surface hundreds of feet, and would have melted the iron in it.

CHAPTER IX.

FINDING OF ROCK IN AND ON ICE.

Arctic explorers have long wondered why rock, gravel, and sand are so often found on and imbedded in bergs and floes.

Many writers claim that rocks are shoved by glaciers, while at the time adhering to them, till the iceberg drifts against another berg and they freeze together. This is not a reasonable explanation how the rocks came on the ice, as the glacier, after it struck the water, would have to turn on its side to bring the bottom of the berg in a position to come in contact with another berg that must have been grounded or become fast in some other manner. Two icebergs, drifting in the ocean, could not freeze together. That would have to be the case if the rocks got into the middle of the berg, where they are frequently found. Besides, how long would a rock, weighing tons, adhere to the bottom or side of an iceberg? No, that is not the way they got there. They were thrown into the air by some explosion, and fell on the berg while it was forming.

Some writers assign one cause, some another; each, however, refutes or rejects what his predecessors have explained of the presence of these substances. To me they appear of volcanic origin. Volcanic eruptions send into the air rock, gravel, sand, and dust, which disperse in every direction. Finally they fall upon the bergs at all stages of formation, from the time the stream first freezes over until a berg is plunged into the ocean, and afterward,— if still in the location where they land. When rock is found on an iceberg, it is stated that it generally rests in a pool of water, caused, it is claimed, by the rock drawing heat from the sun. This does not seem nearly so good an explanation as the one that a warm rock lighting upon an iceberg melts the ice, and makes a pool of water very quickly, there being no need to wait for the sun, which may not appear for several months.

Had I the imagination of Shakespeare, the descriptive power of Homer, and the force and directness of Huxley, then would I paint a picture so vivid and real that no reader of this book would take another view, but would think and see the matter as I do.

We are all limited, however, in our capacity, and must be content to use our gifts as best we may. As soon as one of these facts can be established, the rest must follow. If it can be shown that the rocks found in the icebergs come from an exploding volcano, and that there are no burning volcanoes in the vicinity of the Arctic Ocean, is it not evident, then, that they come from the interior of the earth? When it can also be shown that the conditions are such that no icebergs can be formed on earth, then they must be formed in the interior; for they are certainly formed somewhere. If the material that produces colored snow is a vegetable matter (which the analysis shows), and is supposed to be a blossom or the pollen of a plant, when none such grow in the vicinity of the Arctic Ocean, then it must grow in the interior of the earth; for if it grew elsewhere on earth, then the snow would be colored in other locations as well, which does not seem to be the case.

We might go through a list of more than a dozen hitherto unanswered problems, all pointing in one direction, never conflicting with each other, but each, in turn, strengthening the other, and leaving nothing for the next to explain away. Such a chain of circumstances could not exist on a false theory. Nothing but a fact will stand the test; for facts are stubborn things, and stick out like a sore finger going to a doctor's shop.

The dust, so annoying in the Arctic Ocean, is also produced by volcanic eruptions. Being light, it is carried far away by the wind, and when it falls on the ships is very disagreeable. When it falls with the snow, it produces black snow, and when analyzed, is found to consist of carbon and iron—supposed to come from some burning volcano. Where is that burning volcano? No record or account of any near the North Pole is found, and if it be anywhere else, why does the dust fall in the Arctic Ocean? The best way to dispose of this rock in the ice, this dust in the ocean, this black snow, the shooting stars, or meteors, and the aurora is to say that they are caused by an exploding volcano. I am willing to call that my answer. If false, it will not stand. If true, it will bear the test of time, and pop up like a cork.

As remarked at the beginning of this chapter, one of the mysteries of Arctic travel has always been how rock, gravel, wood, and dirt get on icebergs and ice-drifts. There have been as many explanations as observers: and no two agree. The volcanic-explosion theory would have been of great benefit to those who have written upon this matter when accounting for the rock, etc., being on ice as well as on land. The only difference is that when these substances are on land, they come from a stray comet, passing millions of miles away, and, ninety-nine times out of a hundred, land near the pole. How easy it is to apply the supernatural to matters we do not understand! It is more wonderful to account for a meteor striking the earth, near the pole, from a stray comet a few million miles away, than to have it come from the earth a couple of hundred miles away. Note what Greely says:

"Our traveling was for a long time along the icefoot at the base of very high, precipitous cliffs, evidently of schistose slate. They rose as sheer precipices, over two thousand feet above the level of the bay—solid rock, without a vestige of vegetation to cover their nakedness. Indeed, the only vegetation seen for some ten miles, traveling along these cliffs, was on the outlying spur of clayey earth at the point where our previous camp had been made. In one place a narrow cleft, apparently not more than a hundred feet wide and over a thousand feet deep, broke the continuity of the crest of the bluffs. At one point a rock which must have weighed several tons was lying on a large palæocrystic floe about a half a mile from the shore. I visited and examined it, thinking it might have been brought from some other cliffs, but it was apparently of the same formation as those nearby.   It is worthy of remark that this was the farthest point at which palæocrystic floes were seen in this bay—good evidence that they drifted from the polar ocean."

On page 373 he remarks "that about a mile southwest of the divide Biederbick picked up a piece of lignite coal, which resembles that of The Bellows and of the mines in Watercourse Bay.   It seems somewhat remarkable that this coal is so widely spread over the country and that we should find it on the watershed of Lake Hazen."

Greely did not understand why coal was picked up on the watershed of Lake Hazen. It is not at all strange.   It was dropped there after being thrown into the air by one of those volcanic explosions that produce the beautiful lights hitherto known as the Aurora Borealis, but hereafter to be known as the reflection of fire in the interior of the earth.

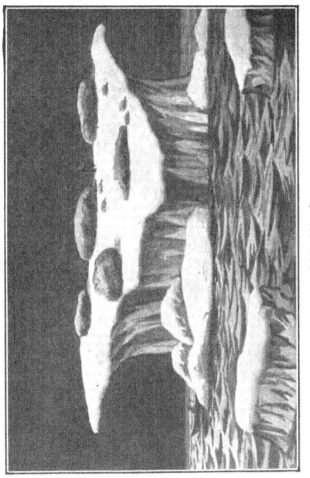

ROCK ON ICE.

The author claims that the rocks shown in the above illustration were thrown into the air by a volcanic explosion, and dropped upon the berg while it was forming.

Kane found masses of detached ice floating out to sea—symmetrical tables two hundred feet long by eighty broad—covered with large angular rocks and boulders, and seemingly impregnated throughout with detrited matter. In Marshall Bay these rafts were so numerous that, could they have melted as he saw them, the bottom of the sea would have presented a more curious study for the geologist than the boulder-covered lines of our middle latitudes.

Hall tells of an old floe, more than twenty feet thick, which grounded near the Polaris. On striking, it broke into many pieces, which, turning over, exposed massive rocks embedded in the ice.

CHAPTER X.

DUST IN THE ARCTIC.

The dust in the polar regions, which Nansen speaks of so many times, and which was a source of such annoyance while drifting in the ocean many miles from land, comes from somewhere; it does not grow; is a commodity without life; cannot reproduce itself; yet it is found in such great quantities that it colors the snow black. In the sky it looks like great clouds, and falls on ships in such abundance that it becomes a source of irritation. Nansen declares it was one of his principal reasons for wanting to go home.

This ought to be accounted for in some reasonable way. So far as I have been able to learn, it is dust from a stray comet, and, when analyzed, is found to contain carbon and iron, supposed to come from some exploding volcano. If it came from a passing comet, it probably started about the same time as the shooting stars, which fall so frequently near the poles! After traveling millions and millions of miles, the dust and shooting stars fall almost continuously; whereas a comet appears only once in several years. Comets must distribute dust and shooting stars sufficient to last till they come again; say, in ten or twenty years. This shows how nonsensical the explanation is; yet, in order to make things clear, it sometimes becomes necessary to show how ridiculous some theories are. This comet theory is most absurd, and does no credit to the first century,—to say nothing of the twentieth.

If it were true that the dust, falling so densely and continuously in the Arctic, came from a comet millions of miles away, the amount necessary to cover the space would shut out the rays of the sun from the earth, which would be veiled in darkness. This dust does not come from a comet; it comes from the earth, and not a great many miles from where it is found.

Dust, as a source of annoyance in the Arctic, is what one would hardly expect in

that region, if the earth be *not hollow.*
Imagine dust as a great annoyance in the
middle of the Arctic Ocean! Nansen
says: "The years are passing here, and
what do they bring? Nothing but dust,
dust, dust, which the first wind drives
away."

Will some one who does not believe
the earth is hollow tell me where that
dust comes from? It isn't an article or
commodity that accumulates very fast on
ice, or open water; yet Nansen says: "Let
us go home; what have we to remain here
for? Nothing but dust, dust, dust."

If you hold that the earth is solid, there
is no answer to this perplexing question.
When it is understood, however, that the
earth is hollow, and the dust comes from
the eruption of a volcano in the interior of
the earth, the puzzle is easily explained
without accusing a passing comet millions
of miles away of scattering dust over all
the Arctic and Antarctic regions. If the
earth is found to be solid, then the people
can congratulate themselves that the dust
is mainly confined to or near the poles,

where the inhabitants are few in number. But there is no danger of that being ever proved.

CHAPTER XI.

OPEN WATER AT FARTHEST POINT NORTH AND SOUTH.

It is still claimed by many that the Arctic Ocean is a frozen body of water. Although it always contains large bodies of drift-ice and icebergs, it is not frozen over. The student of Arctic travels will invariably find that explorers were turned back by open water, and many instances are cited where they came near being carried out to sea and lost. Had they continued going out to sea,—not knowing that the earth was hollow,—they might have been lost but still live. One can easily imagine how those that tried to reach the pole by balloon might get lost and never find their way out, not knowing that the earth was hollow. What I wish to present to the reader, however, is the *proof* that the Arctic Ocean is an open body of water, abounding with game of all kinds, and the farther one advances the warmer

it will be found.   It is never free from
cumulus and dark clouds,—coming up from
the interior of the earth,—and from fogs,
vapors, and other evidences of change.
At certain seasons, when the atmosphere
of the earth at the poles and the atmosphere of the interior of the earth were of
the same temperature, nò clouds would appear unless caused by an eruption of some
kind, which, in many cases, might be
clouds of dust or smoke.

The following extract will afford sufficient proof that my contention on this subject is correct. On page 265, Captain C. F.
Hall says: "On this day (Dec. 26th) Captain Budington speaks in his journal respecting the position of the vessel as follows:

"'On ascending the Providence Iceberg
and taking a look around, we see at first
the open water at a distance of from three
to four miles, extending the whole length
of the strait from north to south.   Our
vessel lies on the edge of the land-floe,
protected from seaward by the iceberg.'"

Here he finds open water to the north,

extending the whole length of the straits from north to south.

Hall further writes, on page 284: "From the top of Providence Berg a dark fog was seen to the north, indicating water. At 10 a. m. three of the men,— Kruger, Nindemann and Hobby,—went to Cape Lupton to ascertain, if possible, the extent of the open water. On their return they reported several open spaces and much young ice—not more than a day old—so thin that it was easily broken by throwing pieces of ice upon it."

Note that he speaks of the dark fog in the north, indicating water, also that they found young ice not more than a day old.

Then, on page 288: "On the 23d of January the two Esquimaux, accompanied by two of the seamen, went to Cape Lupton. They reported a sea of open water extending as far as the eye could reach."

This also was in January: "a sea of open water as far as the eye could reach."

"On the 24th, Dr. Bessels, with two of the seamen, started at 11 a. m., with a dog team, to go north and examine the water reported by the seamen. They reached the third cape without difficulty. Leaving their sled, they arrived at the open water about 2 p. m. They reported a current there running to the north at a rate variously estimated from four miles to a half a mile per hour; at the same hour at the vessel the tide was falling."

Here again on the 24th open water was found, and a current running to the north at a rate variously estimated at from four miles to a half mile per hour; at the same time the tide was falling at the vessel, whereas, according to all established rules, the current should have been going the other way.

Page 289—Hall's diary—has more upon the subject: "On the 28th, Mr. Chester and a small party with dogs and sled, went to inspect the open water which now prevented their rounding the third cape. Mr. Chester observed a current of one mile an hour toward the north. The existence of this open water was regarded as favorable to boat journeys in the spring. A large sled was ordered, upon which one of the boats could be transported to the open water, the extent of which it was proposed to ascertain as soon as possible. Toward evening the sky cleared, and the western coast could be distinctly seen."

Again we have evidence of open water, with the current going north.

Reference to the fog, so frequently referred to by the explorers, is made by Hall, on page 301: "I had for a short time a very extensive view over the straits, where the open water appeared as a dark, black spot on a white field. My joy and pleasure did not, however, last long, as fifteen minutes only sufficed to cover all by a most impenetrable fog, a phenomenon which I never observed before in winter. I was hardly able to see twenty paces to the west and northwest, though toward the south it remained free for a considerable time. There, above the new ice of the bay, a most beautiful fog-stratum, intensely white, was hanging, and continually changing its height."

Being in winter, he calls it a phenomenon. Anything that could cause that fog must be out of the ordinary, and must be accounted for in some other way. If the earth were solid, and the ocean extended to the pole, or connected with land surrounding the pole, there would be nothing to produce that fog. It was caused by the warm air coming from the interior of the earth.

On page 236 Kane says: "Indeed, some circumstances which he (McGary) reports seem to point to the existence of a north water all the year round; and the frequent water-skies, fogs, etc., that we have seen to the S. W. during the winter go to confirm the fact."

He tells us more on the subject (page 299): "Morton's journal, on Monday, the 26th, says: 'As far as I could see the open passages were fifteen miles or more wide, with sometimes mashed ice separating them. But it is all small ice, and I think it either drives out to the open space to the north, or rots and sinks, as I could see none ahead to the north.'

"The coast after passing the cape, he thought, must trend to the eastward, as he

could at no time when below it see any
land beyond.   But the west coast still
opened to the north.

"His highest station of outlook at the
point where his progress was arrested he
supposed to be about three hundred feet
above the sea. From this point, some six
degrees to the west of north, he remarked
in the farthest distance a peak truncated at
its top like the cliffs. of Magdalena Bay.
It was bare at its summit.   This peak, the
most remote northern land known upon
our globe, takes its name from the great
pioneer of Arctic travel, Sir Edward
Parry. * * * The summits were
generally rounded, resembling, to use his
own expression, a succession of sugar-
loaves and stacked cannon-balls declining
slowly in the perspective.   Mr. Morton
saw no ice."

Greely says, on page 150, in reference
to this open-water question: "The cliffs
on the north side of Wrangel Bay were
still washed by the open sea, showing that
the storms of the previous month had
broken up the sea-floe in many places."

Again, on page 254: "This melting of the snow, as well as the limiting clause of Dr. Pavy's orders, prevented him from attempting to proceed northward over the disintegrated pack. He consequently decided to return at once to Cape Joseph Henry. Taking only indispensable effects, and sufficient provisions to feed the party for a few days, they started in haste for the Cape, but on arriving opposite it found open water of three-quarters of a mile in extent between them and the land. On returning to their old camp for some further stores, the water-space toward Cape Hecla was found to have increased in width to about three miles, while the water-clouds to the north and northeast had increased in amount and distinctness."

He does not speak of the increase in amount and distinctness of the water-clouds as one of the signs indicating water in the north, but of an established fact— that the water-cloud (or cloud where the water is reflected in the skies) is no longer a question, but a certainty. It may strike the reader as strange that reference is

made so often to water, ice, and land being
reflected in the sky.   This illustrates that
if the sky correctly reflects at all times the
condition of the water, the ice, and the
land, it will reflect a fire with as much
accuracy as it reflects water.

Dr. Pavy (Greely, page 255) concluded
it unwise to return for some of the
abandoned articles, as the pack was liable
to move northward again, since in the
offing it was drifting south.   He immediately started southward, impressed with
the idea "that Robeson Channel was open,
and that great haste was necessary, fear-
ing that the ice toward Cape Sheridan
would also break up, and seriously delay
their progress homeward."

The ice leading back to their camp was
in better condition than farther north, and
from there they traveled clear back to Lincoln Bay.

"At noon, April 24, the party camped at
View Point, where a record was left in the
old English cairn, and in the evening of
the following day they reached Harley Spit.
At 7 a. m. of the 26th the party was again

in the snow-house at Black Cape. From Cape Sheridan, south of the palæocrystic pack, the ice was broken, in motion, and in many places separated by large lanes of water." The next morning the wind blew from the south, and caused an opening to the north of Black Cape, "between the solid ice of Robeson Channel and the loose floes above—a space of about a mile wide, and of which the transversal end disappeared two or three miles from the coast." The party, however, traveled southward over solid ice to Lincoln Bay.

Despite steady and unremitting labor, and the possession of health and strength, this attempt to travel over the frozen sea failed through natural causes. But, as Dr. Pavy says, it "determined the important fact that last fall open water could have been found as far as Cape Sheridan, and from Conical Hill perhaps to Cape Columbia; and proved, by our experience, that even in such high latitudes the pack may be in motion at an early period of the year; perhaps at any time. I am firmly convinced that but for our misfortune in finding open water, we could, without greatly distancing Commander Markham, have reached perhaps the latitude of 84 deg. N."

Greely writes, on page 275: "We traveled alongside the open river, keeping to the bordering ice-walls, which decreased in thickness and eventually disappeared entirely at a point where the stream doubtless remains open the entire year. Here we were driven to the hillside, where the deep snow and sharp projecting rocks made travel slow, and rendered the task of keeping the sledge upright a severe one. A couple of hundred yards farther and a sharp turn brought in sight a scene which we shall all remember to our dying day. Before us was an immense icebound lake. Its snowy covering reflected 'diamond dust,' from the midnight sun, and at our feet was a broad pool of open, blue water which fed the river. To the northward some eight or ten miles—its base at the northern edge of the lake (Hazen)—a partly snow-clad range of high hills (Garfield Range) appeared, behind and above which the hog-back, snow-clad summits of

the United States Mountains rose with
their stern, unchanging splendor.   To the
right and left on the southern shore low,
rounded hills, bare, as a rule, of snow, extended far to east and west, until in reality
or perspective they joined the curving
mountains to the north.   The scene was
one of great beauty and impressiveness.

"The excitement and enthusiasm which
our new discoveries had engendered, here
culminated, for our vantage ground was
such that all seemed revealed, and no point
hidden.   Connell, who had continually
lamented the frozen foot which turned him
back from the trip to North Greenland, de-
clared enthusiastically that he would not
have missed the scene and discoveries for
all the Polar Sea."

Greely speaks of open water the year
round.   If there be open water the year
round at the farthest point north, can any
good reason be assigned why all have
failed to reach the pole?   The men that
have spent their time, comfort, and, in
several cases, lives, were all men more
than anxious to succeed, yet, strange to

say, all failed.   Was this because the weather got warmer, and they found game more plentiful?   No, it was because there was not such a place.

The following are extracts from Dr. Kane's work, pages 378 and 379: "As far as I could discern, the sea was open, a swell coming in from the northward and running crosswise, as if with a small eastern set.   The wind was due N.—enough of it to make whitecaps—and the surf broke in on rocks below in regular breakers.   The sky to the N. W. was of dark rain-cloud, the first that I had seen since the brig was frozen up.   Ivory-gulls were nesting in the rocks above me, and out to sea were molle-mock and silver-backed gulls.   The ducks had not been seen N. of the first island of the channel, but petrel and gulls hung about the waves near the coast.

"June 26—Before starting, I took a meridian-altitude of the sun (this being the highest northern point I obtained except one, as during the last two days the weather had been cloudy, with a gale blowing from the north), and then set off at

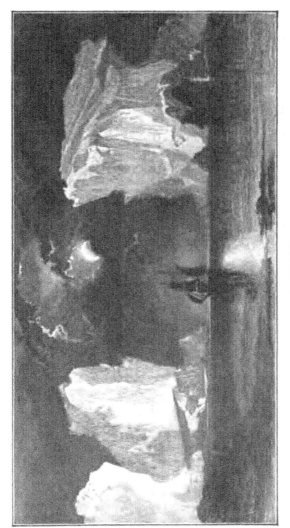

ICEBERGS.

Beautiful scenery, showing the icebergs and ship floating and sailing in open water.

4 p. m. on our return down the channel to
the south.

"I cannot imagine what becomes of the
ice.   A strong current sets in almost constantly to the south; but, from altitudes of
more than five hundred feet, I saw only
narrow strips of ice, with great spaces of
open water, from ten to fifteen miles in
breadth, between them.   It must, therefore, either go to an open space in the
north, or dissolve.   The tides in-shore
seemed to make both north and south; but
the tide from northward ran seven hours,
and there was no slack water.   The wind
blew heavily down the channel from the
open water, and had been freshening since
yesterday nearly to a gale; but it brought
no ice with it."

Dr. Kane says that he cannot imagine
what becomes of the ice, and that it apparently goes to an open space in the north
or dissolves.   Again we read that for
seven hours the tide was from north,
there being no slack water, thus showing
that it did not come from the pole.   If the
tide came from the pole, they should have

had low tide at the expiration of six hours. The tide and wind bringing no ice during all that time, shows plainly enough there was none to bring.

In the second volume of Nansen's work (page 505) more information bears on this point: "I find in my journal for that day: Are continually discovering new islands of lands to the south. There is one great land of snow beyond us in the west, and it seems to extend southward a long way. This snow land seemed to us extremely mysterious; we had not yet discovered a single dark patch on it, only snow and ice everywhere. We had no clear idea of its extent, as we had only caught glimpses of it now and then, when the mist lifted a little. It seemed to be quite low, but we thought it must be of a wider extent than any of the lands we had hitherto traveled along. To the east we found island upon island, and sounds and fiords the whole way along. We mapped it all as well as we could, but this did not help us to find out where we were; they seemed to be only a crowd of small islands, and every now and then a view of what we took to be the ocean to the east opened up between them."

Those islands—passed during the long drift and travel for over a year—were undoubtedly islands that had never been seen before. It is more than likely that Nansen and his crew were farther into the interior than anyone had previously been. If they for one moment could have understood that the earth was hollow, conditions that seemed unexplainable and unaccountable would have been perfectly clear; but as they never dreamed of that, it is not strange that they were constantly mixed, and that currents and winds were always going and coming contrary to customs and theories.

The mist that Nansen speaks of is one strong proof that the earth is hollow and warmer in winter than the exterior.

Changes that are nearly always going on—caused by the wind blowing in or out—must bring about just such effects, as the atmosphere cannot be the same, and is either dryer or more moist, hotter

or colder.   In either case it would be
manifested in some kind of a change—
cloud, fog, snow or rain.

In Vol. I, page 195, Nansen writes of a
fellow-explorer: "In his account of his
voyage, Nordenskiold writes as follows of
the condition of this channel: 'We were
met by only small quantities of that sort of
ice which has a layer of fresh-water ice on
the top of the salt, and we noticed that it
was all melting fiord or river ice.   I hardly
think that we came all day on a single piece
of ice big enough to have cut up a seal
upon.' "

On page 196 of the same volume, occurs:
"We could hardly get on at all for the
dead water, and we swept the whole sea
along with us.   It is a peculiar phenomenon,—this dead water.   We had at present a better opportunity of studying it than
we desired.   It occurs where a surface-
layer of fresh water rests upon the salt
water of the sea, and this fresh water is
carried along with the ship, gliding on the
heavier sea beneath as if on a fixed foundation.   The difference between the two

strata was in this case so great that while we had drinking-water on the surface, the water we got from the bottom cock of the engine room was far too salt to be used for the boiler. Dead water manifests itself in the form of larger or smaller ripples or waves stretching across the wake, the one behind the other, arising sometimes as far forward as almost amidships. We made loops in our course, turned sometimes right around, tried all sorts of antics to get clear of it, but to very little purpose. The moment the engine stopped it seemed as if the ship were sucked back. In spite of the *Fram's* weight and the momentum she usually has, we could in the present instance go at full speed till within a fathom or two of the edge of the ice, and hardly feel a shock when she touched."

I wish to call special attention to Nansen's information about dead water. What is dead water? Does he mean water that has no current? It seems to be one of those phenomena for which they could not account. The only theory that I can present is: the dead water was at a point

where the centre of gravity was extremely
strong; the salt water, being heavier than
the fresh, was drawn to the earth with
such force that the fresh water could not
penetrate it, and laid as separate and distinct upon it as cream upon a pan of milk.
In the absence of any further proof or evidence, this dead water must have been
about half-way round the curve, entering
the interior of the earth, and, if so, was
in perfect accordance with the laws of the
universe—that the centre of gravity is
strongest at this point.

According to Nansen, the ship could
make no headway, and they turned in different directions, and the difference between the strata of salt and fresh water in
this case was so great that while they had
drinking water on the surface, the water
obtained from the bottom cock of the engine room was far too salty to be used for
the boiler. Is there any difference between water found in the Arctic Ocean and
that found in any other ocean? If there
be a difference, what causes it? In New
York harbor we have fresh water and salt

water, but when they meet, they mix. The water that comes down the Hudson River is fresh water, and the water that meets it coming in from the ocean is salt; but there is no line where one may be called fresh, and the other salt. Why should there be a difference, then, in the Arctic Ocean? No other explanation than what I have just stated can be given—that the centre of gravity is so strong near the poles that the heavier body is drawn solidly toward the earth, and the lighter one cannot penetrate it.

Nansen speaks, on page 209, of a different kind of water—a clayey water—where there is no commingling. "To the north of the point ahead of us I saw open water; there was some ice between us and it, but the *Fram* forced her way through. When we got out, right off the point, I was surprised to notice the sea suddenly covered with brown, clayey water. It could not be a deep layer, for the track we left behind us was quite clear. The clayey water seemed to be skimmed to either side by the passage of the ship. I ordered soundings to be taken, and found, as I expected, shallow water—first, eight fathoms, then six and one-half, then five and one-half. I stopped now, and backed. Things looked very suspicious, and round us ice-floes lay stranded. There was also a very strong current running northeast. Constantly sounding, we again went slowly forward. Fortunately the lead went on showing five fathoms. Presently we got into deeper water—six fathoms, then six and one-half, and now we went on at full speed again. We were soon out into the clear, blue water on the other side. There was quite a sharp boundary line between the brown surface and the clear blue. The muddy water evidently came from some river a little farther south."

Many claim that the Arctic Ocean is a frozen body of water; and for that reason considerable space is devoted to the question of open water in the Arctic regions. I contend that the Arctic Ocean is *never* frozen over, although it appears so at different points where large fields of ice have drifted up from the interior of the earth, and lodged at certain places. Nansen spent two years drifting in the Arctic Ocean, which is proof positive that during that time it was not closed by ice. The icebergs that come up from the interior and fill the Arctic Ocean and connecting straits and sounds clear into the Atlantic, cause portions of the Arctic to be filled with ice almost constantly. If it be true that the centre of attraction is strongest at the turning point, large fields of ice would naturally be held in that position, until very strong currents, heavy winds, or large floes coming up from the interior, would shove the ice past that point.

On page 212 of his work Nansen speaks of making such splendid time—eight knots by the log. "Sverdrup thought it would be safer to stay where we were; but it would be too annoying to miss this splendid opportunity; and the sunshine was so beautiful, and the sky so smiling and reassuring! I gave orders to set sail, and soon we were pushing through the ice, under steam, and with every stitch of canvas that

we could crowd on. Cape Chelyuskin
must be vanquished! Never had the *Fram*
gone so fast; she made more than eight
knots by the log; it seemed as though she
knew how much depended on her getting
on. Soon we were through the ice, and
had open water along the land as far as
eye could reach. We passed point after
point, discovering new fiords and islands
on the way, and soon I thought that I
caught a glimpse through a large telescope
of some mountains far away north; they
must be in the neighborhood of Cape Chelyuskin itself."

This was on one of the fifteen days in
succession when Nansen supposed he was
sailing directly north. If he was not sailing north, or nearly so, where was he sailing? He ought to have covered a long
distance, as he speaks of making nine knots
an hour. Had he only made five knots,
the distance would have been nearly 2,000
miles, yet when he took his reckoning he
found himself in latitude 79 degs. If he
had been going straight north, as he supposed he was, his sailing would have taken

him over 1,200 miles past the pole. Allowing for loss of speed, owing to the strength of currents, and dodging bergs and floes, he would still have been beyond the pole.

This is the strongest proof possible that the earth is hollow, and that there is no way of reaching the spot where the North Pole is supposed to be.

On page 217 Nansen writes of one star —the only one to be seen. "It stood straight above Cape Chelyuskin, shining clearly and sadly in the pale sky. As we sailed on and got the cape more to the east of us, the star went with it: it was always there, straight above. I could not help sitting watching it. It seemed to have some charm for me, and to bring such peace. Was it my star? Was it the spirit of home following and smiling to me now? Many a thought it brought to me as the *Fram* toiled on through the melancholy night, past the northernmost point of the old world."

From this, it appears as if he had gone a considerable distance into the interior of the earth—a fact that had something to do,

perhaps, with his seeing only one star. I
hardly think that he was far enough in to
shut out from view all other stars, but his
position would certainly shut out a great
many.

On page 218 he mentions sailing southward to avoid some ice-floes, and making
at the time nine knots an hour. "So that
we were now off King Oscar's Bay; but I
looked in vain through the telescope for
Nordenskiold's cairn. I had the greatest
inclination to land, but did not think that
we could spare the time. The bay, which
was clear of ice at the time of Vegs's visit,
was now closed-in with thick winter ice,
frozen fast to the land. We had an open
channel before us; but we could see the
edge of the drift-ice out at sea. A little
farther west we passed a couple of small
islands, lying a short way from the coast.
We had to stop before noon at the north-
western corner of Chelyuskin, on account
of the drift-ice, which seemed to reach
right into the land before us. To judge
by the dark air, there was open water
again on the other side of an island which

lay ahead. We landed, and made sure
that some straits or fiords on the inside of
this island, to the south, were quite closed
with firm ice; and in the evening the *Fram*
forced her way through the drift-ice on the
outside of it. We steamed and sailed
southward along the coast all night, making splendid way; when the wind was
blowing stiffest, we went at the rate of
nine knots. We came upon ice every now
and then, but got through it easily."

It is apparent that he went a long way
into the interior of the earth.

On page 220 he tells of losing sight of
land entirely. "In the course of the day
we quite lost sight of land, and, strangely
enough, did not see it again; nor did we
see the islands of St. Peter and St. Paul,
though, according to the maps, our course
lay past them."

This statement shows that the explorer
and his men knew nothing about where
they were. If the charts showed that the
islands mentioned above were on the ship's
course, then they were wrong, or Nansen
did not know where he was.

"The channel was still free from ice,"
writes Nansen, on page 225. "We now
continued on our course, against a strong
current, southward along the coast, past
the mouth of the Chatanga. This eastern part of the Taimur Peninsula is a comparatively high, mountainous region, but
with a lower level stretch between the
mountains and the sea, apparently the
same kind of low land we had seen along
the coast almost the whole way. As the
sea seemed to be tolerably open and free
from ice, we made several attempts to
shorten our course by leaving the coast
and striking across for the mouth of the
Olenek; but every time thick ice drove us
back to our channel by the land."

On page 226, Nansen says: "The following day we got into good, open
water, but shallow—never more than
six to seven fathoms. We heard the
roaring waves to the east, so there
must certainly be open water in that
direction, which indeed we had expected.
It was plain that the Lena, with its masses
of warm water, was beginning to assert its

influence. The sea here was browner, and showed signs of some mixture of muddy river water. It was also much less salt."

He found the change so marked that he thought the warm water came from the Lena. Now, the Lena is a river in Siberia, and its waters are no warmer than those of any other river in that country. In certain seasons of the year it discharges a great deal of water, which is not warm enough, however, to have any effect on the Arctic Ocean. Again: the Lena is right on the opposite side of the pole from where Nansen was, and the distance between the two points is considerable.

More concerning this connection is given on page 227. "Saturday, September 16th —We are keeping a northwesterly course (by compass) through open water, and have got pretty well north, but see no ice, and the air is dark to the northward. Mild weather, and water comparatively warm, as high as 35 deg. Fahr. We have a current against us, and are always considerably west of our reckoning. Several flocks of eider-ducks were seen in the course of the day. We ought to have land to the north of us; can it be that which is keeping back the ice?"

The reader will note what he says in regard to their location: "and are always considerably west of our reckoning." So far as knowing their exact position, they were, in fact, lost. If reckoning was taken on the basis that the compass was pointing in a certain direction, when, as a matter of fact, it was pointing in the opposite direction to what they supposed, their reckoning was all wrong. Nansen himself says that they were keeping, by compass, a north-westerly course. Is it not fair to infer that the influence that controlled the compass when Nansen was steering by it, was the same as had controlled it all the time, and that the mixing-up, or confusion, was with the individual, and not the compass?

On page 227 Nansen recounts that they met ice, and supposed, at first, that it would be the end of their journey. However, it was only small drift-ice; and he

states, further, that he had "good sailing
and made good progress."

"Next day we met ice, and had to hold
a little to the south to keep clear of it; and
I began to fear that we should not be able
to get as far as I hoped. But in my notes
for the following day (Monday, September
18th) I read: A splendid day. Shaped
our course northward, to the west of Bielkoff Island. Open sea; good wind from
the west; good progress. Weather clear,
and we had a little sunshine in the afternoon. Now the decisive moment ap-
proaches. At 12.15 shaped our course
north to east (by compass). Now it is
to be proved if my theory, on which the
whole expedition is based, is correct,—if
we are to find a little north from here a
north-flowing current. So far everything
is better than I had expected. We are in
latitude 75½ deg. N., and have still open
water and dark sky to the north and west.
In the evening there was ice-light ahead
and on the starboard bow. About seven I
thought that I could see ice, which, however, rose so regularly that it more resem-

bled land, but it was too dark to see distinctly. It seemed as if it might be Bielkoff Island, and a big light spot farther to the east might even be the reflection from the snow-covered Kotelnoi."

For the previous thirteen days he had found no interruption to speak of, but had continued, as he supposed, steadily north. However, when he took his reckoning he found that he was in latitude 75½ deg. north, and open water still ahead.

On page 228 he remarks that it was a strange feeling to be sailing away north in the dark night to unknown lands, over an open, rolling sea, where no ship or boat had been before. "We might have been hundreds of miles away in more southerly waters, the air was so mild for September in this latitude."

They were surely in the interior of the earth at that point, several miles past the turning point.

Under Tuesday, September 19th (the following day) (page 228), he writes: "I have never had such a splendid sail. On to the north, steadily north, with a good wind, as fast as steam and sail can take us, and open sea mile after mile, watch after watch, through these unknown regions, always clearer and clearer of ice, one might almost say: 'How long will this last?' The eye always turns to the northward as one paces the bridge. It is gazing into the future. But there is always the same dark sky ahead, which means open sea."

The reader will here notice that the appearance of the sky shows the condition of the surface of the earth. This is mentioned to show that when an aurora or a burning fire is reflected in the sky, it should be called a fire, instead of something produced by electricity.

In regard to their good fortune in finding clear sailing direct, as they supposed, toward the pole, Nansen remarks: "Henriksen answered from the crow's-nest when I called up to him. 'They little think at home in Norway just now that we are sailing straight for the pole in clear water.' No, they don't believe we have got so far. And I shouldn't have believed it myself if anyone had prophesied it to me a fortnight ago; but true it is. All my reflections and inferences on the subject had led me to expect open water for a good way farther north; but it is seldom that one's inspirations turn out to be so correct. No ice-lights in any direction, not even now in the evening. We saw no land the whole day; but we had fog and thick weather all morning and forenoon, so that we were still going at half-speed, as we were afraid of coming suddenly on something."

After discussing their good fortune, they again referred to the sky. No ice-lights were in any direction, not even in the evening; but they had thick weather all morning and afternoon, and, as a consequence, were running at half-speed.

"I have almost to ask myself if this is not a dream," writes he on page 230. "One must have gone against the stream to know what it means to go with the stream. As it was on the Greenland expedition, so it is here."

He regards it as such good fortune that he asks himself, "Is it not a dream?" Yet they were no nearer the pole than they were two weeks before.

On the same page he refers to the water: "Hardly any life visible here. Saw an auk or black guillemot to-day, and later a sea-gull in the distance. When I was hauling up a bucket of water in the evening to wash the deck I noticed that it was sparkling with phosphorescence. One could almost have imagined one's self to be in the south."

This is the second time that he notes the phosphorescent water and the fish they caught in that part of the world. In another instance, he stated that, when emptying a net of fish, they looked like glowing embers. This condition of things will be found in many cases, perhaps, in the interior of the earth. Nature provides for every emergency, and it would not be surprising to find phosphorescent effects throughout the interior for the purpose of relieving the darkness. This proved to be nearly Nansen's journey's end; for, on the 21st he met an ice-floe coming up from the interior of the earth, and supposed it to be solid ice in the north. He says (page 233):

"So in the meantime we made fast to a great ice-block, and prepared to clean the boiler and shift coals. We are lying in open water, with only a few large floes here and there; but I have a presentiment that this is our winter harbor."

There is no reason why their progress should have stopped at that point. Anyone on his way to the interior of the earth would not think of such a thing, yet one trying to get to the North Pole might well conclude that that was the commencement of the stopping-place. From this time on to October 12th, nothing of special note occurred.

Three weeks later, he mentions that the water was still open (page 273): "Thursday, October 12th.—In the morning we and our floe were drifting on blue water in the middle of a large, open lane, which stretched far to the north, and in the north the atmosphere at the horizon was dark and blue. As far as we could see from the crow's-nest with the small field-glass,

there was no end to the open water, with
only single pieces of ice sticking up in it
here and there.   These are extraordinary
changes."

He again speaks of "this same dark atmosphere in the north," on page 278, and
"that it indicates open water.   To-day
again, this stretched far away towards the
northern horizon, where the same dark atmosphere indicated some extent of open
water."

On page 282 he speaks of open water to
the north, also the ice-pressure: "Saturday, October 14.—To-day we have got on
the rudder; the engine is pretty well in
order, and we are clear to start north when
the ice opens to-morrow morning.   It is still
slackening and packing quite regularly
twice a day, so that we can calculate on it
beforehand.   To-day we had the same
open channel to the north, and beyond it
open sea as far as our view extended.
What can this mean?   This evening the
pressure has been pretty violent.   The
floes were packed up against the *Fram* on
the port side, and were once or twice on

the point of toppling over the rail. The ice, however, broke below; they tumbled back again, and had to go under us, after all."

On page 291 he is puzzled to know why everything is the reverse of what he had figured it should be. "I had a sounding taken; it showed over seventy-three fathoms (one hundred and thirty-five metres), so we are in deeper water again. The sounding-line indicated that we are drifting southwest. I do not understand this steady drift southward. There has not been much wind either lately; there is certainly a little from the north to-day, but not strong. What can be the reason of it? With all my information, all my reasoning, all my putting of two and two together, I cannot account for any south-going current here—there ought to be a north-going one. If the current runs south here, how is that great, open sea we steamed north across to be explained? and the bay we ended in farthest north? These could only be produced by the north-going current which I presupposed. The only thing which puts me out a bit is that west-going current which we had against us during our whole voyage along the Siberian coast."

What puzzled him was the fact that after he had sailed for fifteen successive days, from September 6 to September 21, with hardly any interruption—what little there was arose mainly from fog—there was so much southerly current and no ice. That would lead to the impression there was no ice to the north, or it would have drifted with the south-going current, and closed the vast body of open water he had sailed through. It is evident the ice in the Arctic, is confined to the floes that come from the interior of the earth. Another evidence that he had advanced far into the interior of the earth, is the quantity of fresh water he met.

Had he known that the earth was hollow, and that they were not sailing north, as he supposed, the answers to these queries would have been clear to him, or the problem have admitted of a different basis of reasoning. He was also going out of salt water; as he says, "the water is not nearly so salt."

On page 338 he is at loss to know why he should find such deep water. "Thursday, December 21.—It is extraordinary, after all, how the time passes. Here we are at the shortest day, though we have no day. But now we are moving on to light, and summer again. We tried to sound to-day; had out twenty-one hundred metres (over eleven hundred fathoms) of line without reaching the bottom. We have no more lines; what is to be done? Who could have guessed that we should find such deep water?"

In rounding the curve of the interior of the earth, as I have said before, it is as likely to be water as land, and is held in position by gravity. I suppose there is, in many cases, practically no bottom, the water being miles and miles deep.

On page 399, under date of Wednesday, February 21st, Nansen says: "The south wind continues. Took up the bag-nets to-day which were put out the day before yesterday. In the upper one, which hung

near the surface, there was chiefly amphipoda; in Murray's net, which hung at
about fifty fathoms' depth, there was a
variety of small crustacea and other small
animals shining with such a strong phosphorescence that the contents of the net
looked like glowing embers as I emptied
them out in the cook's galley by lamplight.
To my astonishment the net-line pointed
northwest, though from the wind there
ought to be a good northerly drift. To
clear this matter up I let the net down in
the afternoon, and as soon as it got a little way under the ice the line pointed
northwest again, and continued to do so
the whole afternoon. How is this phenomenon to be explained? Can we, after
all, be in a current moving northwest?"

Again he is at sea, being unable to account for the current, which is entirely
contrary to what he figured.

On page 309 Kane gives some interesting information on this subject: "This
precipitous headland, the farthest point at-
tained by the party, was named Cape Inde-
pendence. It is in latitude 81 deg. 22 min.

N. and longitude 65 deg. 35 min. W.   It
was only touched by William Morton, who
left his dogs and made his way to it along
the coast.   From it the western coast was
seen stretching far towards the north, with
an iceless horizon, and a heavy swell rolling in with whitecaps.   At a height of
about five hundred feet above the sea this
great expanse still presented all the appearance of an open and iceless sea.   In
claiming for it this character I have reference only to the facts actually observed,
without seeking confirmation or support
from any deduction or theory.   Among
such facts are the following:

"1. It was approached by a channel
entirely free from ice, having a length of
fifty-two and a mean width of thirty-six
geographical miles.

"2. The coast-ice along the water-line
of this channel had been completely de-
stroyed by thaw and water action, while
an unbroken belt of solid ice, one hundred
and twenty-two miles in diameter, extended to the south.

"3. A gale from the northeast, of fifty-

NORTHERN ENTRANCE.

Globe showing entrance to the interior of the earth at
the North Pole.

four hours' duration, brought a heavy sea from that quarter, without disclosing any drift or other ice.

"4. Dark *nimbus* clouds and water-sky invested the northeastern horizon.

. "5. Crowds of migratory birds were observed thronging its waters."

Nansen, in Vol. II, pages 534 and 535, says: "We now found that in March he must have been at no great distance south of our winter hut, but had to turn there, as he was stopped by open water—the same open water of which we had seen the dark atmosphere all the winter."

Herein he refers to Jackson, who found him after his long trip on the ice with Johansen. After leaving the *Fram,* this open water that kept them apart was seen by Nansen in the skies all winter, whenever the atmosphere was favorable.

Now, what are the conditions obtaining in the Antarctic region? Louis Bernacchi, who spent nearly two years in the extreme southern portion, tells us:

"At Cape Adare huge bergs were often observed during perfectly calm weather, traveling at about four knots per hour toward the northwest." (Page 39.)

"In this open sea is where they meet so many icebergs."

"An open sea, comparatively free from ice, is met with in the Antarctic regions."

He declares an open sea can be found. If so, why do they not reach the pole? He tells us that they passed the magnetic pole. They did; and had they kept on, instead of turning back for fear of being lost at sea, they would have made a great discovery.

But I am in favor of entering the interior of the earth from the north, on account of the apparently high winds in the Antarctic. I also am of the opinion that Mount Erebus—from which Bernacchi saw smoke coming—is in the interior of the earth, or part of the way in.

After the foregoing evidence, is it possible that anyone can believe that the respective oceans are frozen bodies of water? If they do not believe that these oceans are frozen, why do the explorers fail to reach the poles—if there be such places?

CHAPTER XII.

WHY IT IS WARMER NEAR THE POLES.

One of the principal proofs that the earth is hollow, is that it is warmer near the poles. If this be so, to what are we to attribute the heat? Nothing, however, has been found to produce heat near the poles to make it warmer. If it can be shown—by quoting those who made the farthest advance toward the supposed poles—that it is warmer, that vegetation shows more life, that game is more plentiful than farther south, then we have a reasonable right to claim that the heat comes from the interior of the earth, as that seems to be the only place from which it could come. In presenting the reports of those best able to judge, very little comment will be made, as the reader should form his own opinions.

In "Captain Hall's Last Trip," page 166, is read: "We find this a much warmer

country than we expected. From Cape
Alexander the mountains on either side
of the Kennedy Channel and Robeson's
Strait we found entirely bare of snow and
ice, with the exception of a glacier that we
saw covering, about latitude 80 deg. 30
min., east side the strait, and extending
east-northeast direction as far as can be
seen from the mountains by Polaris Bay.

"We have found that the country
abounds with life, and seals, game, geese,
ducks, musk-cattle, rabbits, wolves, foxes,
bears, partridges, lemmings, etc. Our
sealers have shot two seals in the open
water while at this encampment. Our
long Arctic night commenced October
13th, having seen only the upper limb of
the sun above the glacier at meridian October 12th."

Nansen draws special attention to the
warmth, for he says: "Fancy, only 12 deg.
(21½ deg. Fahr.) of frost in the middle
of December! We might almost imagine
ourselves at home—forget that we were
in a land of snow to the north of the
eighty-first parallel."

This was at one of the farthest points
north reached by anyone, only in a different direction; and yet the weather was
mild and pleasant.

Peary also makes mention of the higher

PTARMIGAN.
Birds found in great numbers in the Arctic Circle.

temperature. On pages 214 and 215, he
says: "I expected to hear later of our
February fohn in other parts of Greenland,
and I was not disappointed. Lieutenant
Ryder was living for nine months at
Scoresby Sound, on the coast of East

Greenland, while we were at McCormick
Bay.   He was about four hundred and
fifty geographical miles south of us.   The
maximum temperatures he recorded occurred in February and May.   He says
(Petermann's Mittheilungen, XI, 1892,
page 256) that these high temperatures
were due to severe fohn storms, one of
which, in February (date not given), suddenly raised the thermometer to 50 deg.
F., 8½ deg. higher than my instrument had
recorded."

It will be observed that these extremely
strong winds from the interior of the earth
not only raise the temperature considerably in the vicinity of the Arctic Ocean,
but affect it very materially four hundred
and fifty miles away.   Nothing could
raise the temperature in such a manner,
except a storm coming from the interior
of the earth.

Nansen, in his second volume, page 355,
tells us: "This island we came to seemed
to me to be one of the most lovely spots on
the face of the earth.   A beautiful flat
beach, an old strand lined with shells

strewn about, a narrow belt of clear water along shore, where snails and sea urchins (Echinus) were visible at the bottom and amphipoda were swimming about. In the cliffs overhead were hundreds of screaming little auks, and beside us the snow-buntings fluttered from stone to stone with their cheerful twitter. Suddenly the sun burst forth through the light, fleecy clouds, and the day seemed to be all sunshine. Here was life and fair land; we were no longer on the eternal drift-ice! At the bottom of the sea just beyond the beach I could see whole forests of seaweed (Laminaria and Fucus). Under the cliffs here and there were drifts of beautiful rose-colored snow."

When one takes into account Nansen's description of this island, and connects that with the fact that no one has been able to reach the pole, notwithstanding that the travelers keep going where it is warmer, where there is more life, less ice, and but little snow, yet they make no progress that leads them to the much-sought goal, this is one of the strongest arguments that there is no such place. The farther the explorers pass into the interior of the earth, the warmer it will be found; and when they succeed in passing the belt of country that has so much fog, snow, and clouds, and drift-ice coming up from the interior, they will find plain sailing and comfortable weather, but they will never reach the pole.   Whoever spends his time and strength looking for the poles will be like a young doctor in Illinois.   Some one told him that the milk-sickness was very bad in a certain county in that State, and he, not having much practice, thought he would like to try his hand at curing it. He started for the county where it was reported to be the worst, but when he got there he was told that there was no milk-sickness in that county, but it was quite bad in the county adjoining.   So he traveled on, and when he got there, they told him the same story.   After chasing the phantom for a while, he returned, and reported that it was harmless, as no disease need be feared when no one could get nearer to it than the county adjoining.

That is much nearer than explorers will ever get to the poles.

On one of Greely's farthest trips north —of which he gives an account on page 73—he speaks of the vegetation: "This creek was of moderate size, and drained a valley of considerable extent, which extended to the northwestward. The vegetation seemed more abundant than at Cape Hawks, and eight varieties of flowers were gathered during our brief stay, but the general appearance was of desolation."

This shows that it was getting warmer.

Again, on the same trip out from camp to explore the surroundings, he speaks of a large flock of eider-ducks that had settled in an open pool, and to the north, three-quarters of a mile, ten musk-oxen were quietly grazing; the sloping hills were covered with vegetation, flowers, the familiar buttercup, and countless Arctic poppies of luxuriant growth. "Surely this presence of birds and flowers and beasts was a greeting on nature's part to our new home."

Does that sound as if he had expected to

find these things there, or that their presence was an everyday occurrence? No:
it is the tone of surprise.

From what place had those birds and

EIDER-DUCKS.
Found in great numbers in the Arctic Circle.

game come? South of them for many
miles the earth is covered with a perpetual
snow—in many locations thousands of feet
deep. They are found in that location in
summer; and as it is warmer farther north,

they would not be likely to go to a colder climate in winter. They seem to pass into the interior of the earth, or as far as suits their nature. Let me state here that the mutton-birds of Australia leave that continent in September, and no one has ever been able to find out where they go. My theory is that they pass into the interior of the earth, via the South Pole.

Greely says again, on page 264: "While we were at this camp, Private Connell visited the mouth of the valley running to the northwest. He found vegetation to be abundant, and reported that during the summer months a river evidently flows into the bay from the valley. At that point he also noted four wolves, and with them a musk-ox, the first of the season. Leading to the valley, he also found what appeared to be a musk-ox trail (similar to the buffalo trails of the 'Far West'), which indicated plainly the valley was a winter resort for these animals."

As they proceeded farther north, where no white man had ever trod, they found the trails of musk-ox, showing that those animals made it their winter abode. Remember, they had traveled hundreds of miles without meeting any signs of life.

"As we were about entering camp, a dark-colored bird, about the size of a plover, flew swiftly by us from behind, and disappeared. It was neither snow-bunting nor ptarmigan, as all agreed. Wolf, fox, lemming, hare, musk-ox, and ptarmigan tracks were all seen during the day." (Page 276.)

On page 330, he says: "This camp proved prolific in animal life, thus indicating a luxuriant vegetation near. Two ptarmigan were flying around, a hare was captured, and traces of foxes and lemmings were observed. Tracks of a passing bear, going to the northeast, were seen on the ice-foot, and abundant traces of musk-oxen were discovered, proving that these animals frequent this place in considerable numbers, though the indications were not of recent date."

"Sergeant Brainard, who had charge of the fresh meat, records that up to this date fifty-two musk-oxen had been obtained in

1882, averaging two hundred and forty-
three pounds each of dressed meat."
(Page 422.)

"Long returned at 6 p. m., having been
gone twenty-two hours hunting.   His pro-
longed absence caused much alarm, as he
was alone.   Several parties had been sent
out to seach for him, when he was met returning.   He had fallen in with a herd of
musk-oxen in the valley, about two miles
above the head of St. Patrick Bay.   He
had sixteen rounds of ammunition at starting, and, shortly after, fired two at an
owl.   With the remaining ammunition he
killed eight musk-oxen, and wounded two
others; four escaped.   He had delayed to
skin the eight before returning to the station, in order that the meat should not
taint.   He saw three large falcons, the
first that had been observed by us."

The skinning of the musk-oxen by
Long, to prevent tainting of the flesh,
would naturally suggest unusually warm
weather to the reader.   While the weather
was warm, that was not the only reason
why the animals were immediately

skinned. If the musk-ox is left any length of time after death with the skin on, the meat becomes tainted, regardless of weather conditions.

Where could one go and find such abundance of game as at the farthest point north reached? The game is found there in summer. Can anyone tell where it goes in winter? Greenland is covered with snow from one to ten thousand feet deep. (Vide Peary's report of his trip to the Arctic overland.) If the game be found at the extreme northerly points in summer, is it reasonable to suppose it would migrate to a colder climate in winter? It would be better to stay where it is. Greely tells us that the trails indicate that the musk-oxen make their winter quarters there. Since it becomes warmer as they go north, instinct tells them not to go south in winter. And if they do not go south, they must go into the *interior* of the *earth*.

Nansen (Vol. II, page 75) gives us a description of the conditions that obtained, from which one can judge of the warmth

of the weather: "I cannot help believing
that a land which, even in April, teems
with bears, auks, and black guillemots, and
where seals are basking on the ice, must be
a Canaan, flowing with milk and honey,

SHOOTING SEALS.
How natives slaughter seals in the Arctic Circle.

for two men who have good rifles and good
eyes; it must surely yield food enough not
only for the needs of the moment, but also
provisions for the journey onward to
Spitzbergen."

This was Nansen's remark when he was

about to leave the *Fram,* after he had drifted nearly five months in an ice-floe.

In the same volume, page 346, he gives additional evidence as to weather and warmth. "It is a curious sensation to paddle in the mist, as we are doing, without being able to see a mile in front of us. The land we found we have left behind us. We are always in hopes of clear weather, in order to see where the land lies in front of us—for land there must be. This flat, unbroken ice must be attached to land of some kind; but clear weather we are not to have, it appears. Mist without ceasing; we must push on as it is."

The mist, fog, and clouds spoken of as so prevalent, should be accounted for by something different than plain Arctic Ocean. The best explanation seems that warm air comes from the interior of the earth (where the atmosphere is wholly different), and when it passes out in winter produces mist, fog, or cloud; but more generally snow, summer or winter.

Nansen, in Volume II, page 354, says: "As I mentioned before (August 13), I had at first supposed the sound on our west to be Rawlinson's Sound, but this now appears impossible, as there was nothing to be seen of Dove Glacier, by which it is bounded on one side. If this was now our position, we must have traversed the glacier and Wilczek Land without noticing any trace of either; for we have traveled westward a good half degree south of Cape Buda-Pesth. The possibility that we could be in this region we consequently now hold to be finally excluded. We must have come to a new land in the western part of Franz Josef Land, or Archipelago, and so far west that we had seen nothing of the countries discovered by Payer. But so far west that we had not even seen anything of Oscar's Land, which ought to be situated in 82 deg. North and 52 East. This was indeed incomprehensible; but was there any other explanation?"

And this is Nansen's experience after traveling and drifting more than a year on floating ice, when he undoubtedly passed farther into the interior than any explorer, although he himself did not know where he was.

Schwatka speaks of the game in the Arctic region. After reading, the reader will naturally ask where it goes during the winter. Some say that it goes south; but where does it stop? I know of no place where such an amount of game goes in winter. Most of the game that Schwatka mentions is certainly not at all common to any location I can think of; or, if so, the number must be limited. I am quite sure that the game passes into the interior of the earth, as many of the birds are heavy, and not built for long journeys.

"In no place in the world," says Schwatka, "is aquatic life so abundant as in the polar regions during the summer. The instance I have given of the eiders in Terror Bay is but one of many constantly encountered in polar literature. 'The little auks or rotges,' says a writer who has been in Spitzbergen, 'are so numerous that I have frequently seen an uninterrupted line of them extending to a distance of more than three miles, and so close to-

A SWARM OF AUKS,

These birds are found so plentiful in the Arctic regions that when they fly overhead they darken the skies, their little voices being often heard from a distance of four or five miles.

gether that thirty have fallen at one shot.'
This living column might be about six
yards broad and as many deep, so that,
allowing sixteen birds to the cubic yard,
there would be four millions of these little
creatures on the wing at one time. This
number may appear greatly exaggerated,
but when we are told that these auks con-
gregate in such swarms as to darken the
air like a passing cloud, and that their
chorus is heard distinctly at a distance of
four or five miles, these numbers do not
appear so great. The dovekies are the
most numerous of the summer ducks in
the northern part of the bay, and they are
especially thick about Depot Island, whose
Innuit name is Pikkeulik, meaning the isl-
and of birds' nests, and where the dovekies deposit their greenish, blotched eggs
in innumerable quantities."

Kane narrates, page 301, that "after
traveling due north over a solid area
choked with bergs and frozen fields, Morton was startled by the growing weakness
of the ice, its surface becoming rotten, and
the snow wet and pulpy. His dogs, seized

with terror, refused to advance. Then
for the first time the fact broke upon him
that a long, dark band seen to the north
beyond a protruding cape—Cape Andrew
Jackson—was water. With danger and
difficulty he retraced his steps and, reaching sound ice, made good his landing on
a new coast."

On page 302 Kane adds: "From the
southernmost ice, seen by Dr. Hayes only
a few weeks before, to the region of this
mysterious water was, as the crow flies,
one hundred and six miles. But for
the unusual sight of birds and the unmis-
takable giving way of the ice beneath them
they would not believe in the evidence of
eyesight. Neither Hans nor Morton was
prepared for it. Landing on the cape,
and continuing their exploration, new phenomena broke upon them. They were on
the shores of a channel, so open that a
frigate, or a fleet of frigates, might have
sailed up it. As they traveled north, this
channel expanded into an iceless area;
for four or five small pieces—lumps
—were all that could be seen over the en-

tire surface of its whitecapped waters.
Viewed from the cliffs, and taking thirty-
six miles as the mean radius open to reliable survey, this sea had a justly estimated extent of more than four thousand
square miles."

In the above excerpt, Kane speaks of
traveling one hundred and six miles
due north, over solid ice, to open water,
and finding it filled with all kinds of game,
of which there had been no sign one hundred and six miles farther south. How
is this accounted for on the theory that
the earth is solid? If it was becoming
warmer, what made it so? If the winds,
blowing in from a still colder climate,
would produce a warm atmosphere, then
all I have to say is that Nature operates
differently at the poles than elsewhere on
earth. A hot breeze cannot blow off an
iceberg any more than a cold breeze can
belch out of a red-hot furnace. The fact
is, the earth being hollow, the air passes
out of the interior of the earth; hence
the interior atmosphere is necessarily
warmer.

CHAPTER XIII.

DRIFTWOOD—WHENCE IT CAME.

The driftwood and other material found on the northern sides of the shores bordering the Arctic Ocean, present further proof that the earth is hollow, and that the material came from the interior of the earth; some say from Siberia. If so, and it floated from there, it must have come past the supposed pole. Why, then, cannot the explorers sail over the very same course?

Because the driftwood never came from there; if it had, they could have pursued the same route. One might ask why they have not explored, or sailed, to the place from which this driftwood came. Heretofore, all explorers have had but one object in view,—to get as far north as possible, not knowing that the earth was hollow. If the compass told anything after they got half-way round, or more, it would locate the north from the place they had just come from (having passed the magnetic pole) ; and, not aware, therefore, that it was the compass, and not the ship, that had turned round, they would steer out again, thinking they were going north. It would be next to impossible to reach the interior of the earth under such conditions, passing through stormy, cloudy, and foggy weather, and not knowing how the compass should work.

Greely tells us, on page 100, that Private Connell and Frederick found a large coniferous tree on the beach just above the extreme high-water mark. It was about thirty inches in circumference, some thirty feet long, and had apparently been carried within a couple of years to that point by a current. A portion of it was cut up for firewood, and for the first time in that valley a bright, cheery camp-fire gave comfort to man. Now, there is no timber of the dimensions mentioned growing anywhere near where it was found. Whence did it come? There is but one place that I can think of, and that is the interior of the earth. A wood fire made from native wood is a thing practically unknown, barring a few dry willows.

Farther on (page 106), Greely states that a large number of pieces of driftwood were found near or slightly above the high-water mark. Some of the pieces were six or seven feet long, and from four to eight inches in diameter. Nearly all were coniferous woods. If this wood drifted from the earth's surface, it would be obliged to go hundreds of miles, and almost constantly through frozen water; while, upon the other hand, if it came from the interior of the earth, it would have open water to drift in, and tidal waves to lift it above the high-water mark.

On page 308 Greely informs us that about half a mile from the coast he found an old piece of driftwood nearly six feet long, four inches wide, and four inches thick—apparently pine or fir, and evidently split from the body or branch of a tree. It was partly buried, and indications were that the tree must have been large.

Note that he speaks of it as *partly* buried,

which would be the case if it had been thrown there by some volcanic eruption.

One of the most interesting articles he discovered was a piece of birch bark, admirably preserved. This timber; it should be noted, never grows in that vicinity.

On page 368 Greely says: "On the shores of this lake Biederbick found a pair of reindeer antlers, and I picked up a piece of close-grained wood—apparently pine—two and a half feet long, and nearly an inch in diameter. In a ravine near the camp were two trees, probably coniferous, partly covered by earth. One was ten feet long and sixteen inches in diameter, and originally had two branches. The second tree was six feet long and twelve inches in diameter. They were about one hundred and fifty yards distant from Lake Heintzelmann."

If Greely was in a country where such timber grew, why did he say anything about it? Because it did *not* grow in that country, the incident was worth recording.

Greely writes on page 370 of the many musk-oxen—fifteen in one herd and three in another—which he saw. In the vicinity enough willow remained to enable them to make a fire and brew tea.

From the writings of different explorers, I learn that willow is about the only shrub or timber growing in that country. It sprouts in the spring, and is generally frozen down in the winter, and it is unusual to have it large enough to cook a cup of tea; so much so that he speaks of it in this connection.

Nansen says, on page 303: "A secret doubt lurked behind all the reasoning. It seemed as though the longer I defended my theory, the nearer I came to doubting it. But no, there is no getting over the evidence of that Siberian driftwood."

Although Nansen felt the driftwood came from Siberia, I hold an entirely different view: it came from the interior of the earth.

CHAPTER XIV.

HAVE OTHER THAN THE ESKIMOS INHAB-
ITED THE ARCTIC REGIONS?

I am of the opinion that another race besides Eskimos have dwelt in the Arctic regions, and may still live, perhaps, in the interior of the earth. If so, one cannot but think that their civilization was of a low order—if they could be called civilized at all—from the fact that little is or has been found to show that they were skilled in building. If they were at all adept, or had made some slight advance, some of the drift from the Arctic would have shown how far they had progressed. From what Greely discovered, it is safe to conclude that if the interior of the earth be peopled, it is by a race something akin to that now found in the Arctic Circle. Extracts from Greely bearing on this subject will be found hereinafter.

On page 379 he writes that he was greatly surprised to discover, against a

vertical bank facing Ruggles River, three
abandoned Eskimo huts, which doubtless
had been occupied in the far past as permanent abodes. "These houses were
built from large, fine pieces of slate, which
were readily obtainable from the adjoining rocks. Many pieces of this slate, as
large as three feet by two feet, were lying
around, the thickness of which varied
from three-quarters of an inch to an inch
and a half. The Eskimo had utilized the
steep precipitous bank against which the
back of the houses rested, and in which the
chimneys were built. The houses were
six feet wide and ten feet long, though
possibly they may have been longer, as
the walls most distant from the bank had
fallen and partly disappeared, through being undermined by the river. The side-
walls of the structure were about three
feet in height. Apparently the whole
house had been covered with large pieces
of slate, which served as a roof, for many
such pieces were found in the interior
space, which was partly filled by them.
It is probable that the width of the houses

depended on the size of the pieces of slate which could be used as a covering. No signs of a ridge-pole, or a wooden support to the roof, were to be seen. We carefully removed the flat slabs, and, digging among the dirt and moss, which was of considerable depth, found many relics and bones, which were most numerous near the chimney, or fireplace. Bones of the musk-ox, hare, and of various birds (and at least one kind of fish) were found in great abundance. Among other articles were three combs of walrus ivory, one of which had ornamental work on it, and whalebone fish-hooks, a bone needle, and pieces of whalebone, a shoe for a sledge-runner, and a number of other worked articles of bone and wood, the use of which was unknown. A selection was made from the bones, in order that it might be determined what species of animals had been killed by the Eskimo who had occupied this place. A piece of dog-skin of considerable size was also dug-out, which had rotted to such an extent that it fell to pieces when handled."

Farther on, he says: "In the two houses and in the immediate vicinity we collected about forty pieces of wood and worked bone. Among other articles were one large and two small narwhal horns, two walrus ivory toggles for dog-traces, such as are now used by the Greenlanders; an arrow-head, two bone handles, a skinning-knife with bone handle and iron blade, a bear's tooth, whalebone shoes for the runners of two sledges, and a wooden up-stander with a carefully made and well-fitted bone top. Several sledge-bars, some of bone and others of wood, and a complete wooden sledge-runner, which was very heavy, being five feet long, nine inches high, and over two inches thick, were also discovered.

"Among other pieces of wood was a pole, nine feet long, and about two inches in diameter, of a hard, close-grained, coniferous wood, probably fir or hard pine. Parts of two wooden sledge-runners were badly rotted, but one was yet in fair condition.

"There were several articles of worked

bone whose use I could not surmise, and the character of which was unknown to our own Eskimo. The bone articles were of walrus, narwhal and whalebone, the first being the predominating material, from which small articles had been made. Musk-ox and hare bones were very plentiful.

"It appears evident, my Journal says, that these Eskimos had dogs, sledges, arrows, and skinning knives, and fed on musk-oxen, seals, hares, and occasionally fish. While this habitation does not appear to have been covered with stones, as were those found by me on the east side of the river, yet the arrangements indicate more than a summer encampment.

"It is more than probable that these habitations were covered with skin roofs, which must have been secured in a different manner from the Greenland method, as no circles of stones were found. The construction of these houses certainly entailed a large amount of work. In quitting them, the roof and its supports must have been entirely removed. It is possible that the long pole found may have been used in some manner as a support for the roof. It is extraordinary that, in abandoning this country, they should have left behind the pole and the sledges, which were very valuable, unless, indeed, their dogs perished there. The depth at which the dog-toggles and other articles were discovered indicates their having been left by accident where found, as they were covered by débris, which evidently accumulated during the occupancy of these huts.

"The surroundings were carefully examined for graves, as during the occupancy, covering at least two years, of habitations of such size, it was likely some one must have died. No traces of any human remains could be found, nor, indeed, of the dogs; but, in the case of the latter, their uncared-for remains would have been devoured and their bones removed by foxes or wolves. It is pertinent to remark that musk-ox or other expected bones were rarely found in Grinnell Land. Nearly an hour was spent in the examination of these remains, after which we started westward."

On page 420 Greely again writes: "Sergeant Brainard—who seemed intuitively to locate such places—discovered the sites of eighteen Eskimo summer tents, and gathered near them a large number

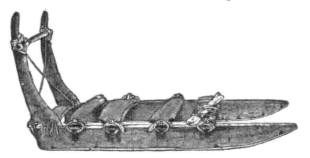

Sled found by Greely during one of his trips farthest north.

of relics.   The circles varied from five to fifteen feet in diameter.   There were two upstanders, runners, bone shoes, crossbars, etc., making a complete sledge; a very large stone (steatite, probably) lamp, fifteen inches across, was broken in five pieces, and had been fastened together by seal thongs.   There   was   also   a   bone

spear-head, and other relics of like material, the use of which was unknown to our
Danish Eskimo."

CHAPTER XV.

WHAT PRODUCES COLORED SNOW IN THE ARCTIC?

Why is the snow colored in the Arctic regions?   What causes it to be colored?

The snow has been analyzed, and the red, green, and yellow have been found to contain vegetable matter, presumably a flower, or the pollen of a plant.   The black snow has also been analyzed, and found to contain carbon and iron, supposed to come from a volcanic eruption.   But whence did it come?   A flower that produced pollen sufficient to permeate the air with such density that it colored the snow, would require a vast territory— millions of acres—to grow it.   Where is that to be found?   If on earth, it must be near the North Pole; for, if it grew elsewhere, colored snow would be found at other locations, and not be confined to the Arctic regions.   As no such flowering plant is known on earth, we must look elsewhere.

The interior of the earth is the only spot that will furnish us with an answer to the question. As the colors fall at different seasons, it is fair to presume that the flower matures at those seasons. It is also easy to find out where the black snow, frequently mentioned by the explorers, comes from. It comes out of an exploding volcano—of the kind that covered Nansen's ship with dust. All unexplained questions could be easily answered if one would believe that the earth is hollow; it is impossible to answer them under any other theory. A falsehood could not furnish so many solutions: one or two might point to some other answer; but a score of unanswered problems could not be answered by a falsehood.

Kane, in his first volume, page 44, says: "We passed the 'Crimson Cliffs' of Sir John Ross in the forenoon of August 5th. The patches of red snow, from which they derive their name, could be seen clearly at the distance of ten miles from the coast.

It had a fine, deep-rose hue, not at all like the brown stain which I noticed when I was here before. All the gorges and ravines in which the snow had lodged were deeply tinted with it. I had no difficulty now in justifying the somewhat poetical nomenclature which Sir John Franklin applied to this locality; for if the snowy surface were more diffused, as it is no doubt earlier in the season, crimson would be the prevailing color."

Kane also states: "The red snow was diversified with large surfaces of beautifully green mosses and alopecurus; and where the sandstone was bare, it threw in a rich shade of brown."

Kane speaks of the red snow as if it had a regular season in which to appear—as he says "if the snowy surface were more diffused, as it is no doubt earlier in the season." In another place he speaks of the red snow being two weeks later than usual. Now, taking the fact into account that the material that colors the snow is a vegetable matter, supposed to be the blossom or pollen of a plant, and that no such plant grows on earth, where does it come from? The time for its appearance is in July and August. This may not seem of great importance to many readers, but when taken in connection with the object of this book, then it becomes important; for if it does not grow on the earth, it must grow in the interior of the earth.

CHAPTER XVI.

WHERE AND HOW ARE ICEBERGS FORMED?

As already stated, it is impossible for an iceberg to form at any place where it is warmest at the mouth of the stream or cañon. If it be warmer at the mouth than farther inland, the mouth would be the last to freeze over, and there would be no water to pass over the ice to make an iceberg. If one *was formed*—it being warmer at the mouth—it would commence to thaw there first, and where would water come from to break it loose and push it into the ocean? It could not start until the whole length of the river was thawed loose, and would then have to come down as a whole, as there would be nothing to break it. It is simply out of the question for an iceberg to form in any location yet discovered. On the other hand, the interior of the earth—back from the mouth of the rivers or cañons—being warmer, is just suited for the formation of icebergs. The mouth freezes first, and the river, continuing to flow to the ocean, overflows the mouth, and freezes for months, until spring. As the warm weather of summer advances, and, owing to the warmth from the earth, the bergs are thawed loose, the water from the rains in the interior rushes down, they are shoved into the ocean, and tidal waves are started.

Note the difference. On earth, the whole length of a stream is frozen, and the farther inland the harder the freezing, while in the interior only the mouth is frozen, and the open water is well supplied with rains to produce the bergs. In the interior of the earth, also, there is not only plenty of water to produce these bergs, but plenty to shove them into the ocean, while on earth there isn't water for either purpose.

For the last three hundred years a fairly steady stream of explorers have been trying to reach the poles—Arctic and Antarctic—and the shores of the Arctic region have been traveled by thousands, including the natives, yet no one has ever seen an iceberg leaving its original location, and plunging into the ocean. The reason that mention of such an occurrence has never been recorded is that it has never been seen. Hall, it is true, reports having seen a landslide, and Kane saw a large piece of ice break from a projecting cliff; but not an iceberg. Yet bergs are so numerous, that the oceans are full of them. Isn't it strange that no one has thought of asking about the place of their origin? No, it is not so strange when one stops to think that heretofore the general belief has been that the earth is solid, and that the icebergs must come from some location near the poles.

What is to be found in the Antarctic Ocean to bear out the theory that icebergs come from the interior of the earth, and cannot be formed on earth? Bernacchi says: "There was less than two inches of rainfall in eleven and one-half months, and while it snowed quite frequently, it never fell to any great depth."

Under those conditions, where would

materials be found to produce an iceberg? Yet the greatest one on earth is there—one so large that it is called the Great Ice Barrier, rather than an iceberg—being over four hundred miles long and fifty miles wide. It is grounded in two thousand one hundred feet of water, and extends from eighty to two hundred feet above water.

Now, it would be impossible for this berg to form in a country having practically no rain or snow. As icebergs are made from frozen water, and there is no water to freeze, it evidently was formed at some place other than where it now is; the berg itself, being of fresh water, lies in mid-ocean of salt water.

"Where could such an iceberg be formed?" In the interior of the earth; in a long, wide, deep, and straight river. How do I know this? Just as I know anything that I have not seen, or that has not yet come to pass. How do I know that the temperature next July will be warmer than it was last January? Because one of the great laws of the universe declares it shall be so. We get our heat from the sun, and next July the earth will be directly opposite to it; therefore the rays of the sun will strike the United States more squarely. In January the sun strikes the United States slanting, or obliquely, and we do not get so much heat. That is why *I know this* Barrier was formed in the interior of the earth.

Again, how do I know that that Great Ice Barrier came from the interior of the earth, and from the kind of river described? First, it could not come from the earth, as icebergs are not formed on earth. Second, the river that that berg was frozen in must have been twenty-five hundred feet deep, fifty miles across, and from four to five hundred miles long: for those are the present dimensions of the berg: the river had to be straight, or the berg could not have passed out without breaking. It passed through a comparatively level country, for the surface is still flat. Probably the berg took thousands of years to freeze, and was released only when some burning volcano reached a point near enough to thaw it loose; heavy rains then shoved it to its present location.

Another proof that the interior of the earth is level near the Antarctic entrance, is that many of the icebergs found in the Antarctic are long and slim. They are called "ice-tongues," which indicates that they came out of rivers running nearly on a level. The bergs found in the Arctic, on the other hand, are more chunky, indicating that they come from a more mountainous country, where the fall of streams is more abrupt, causing the bergs to be shorter and probably thicker.

Should anyone ask why Livingstone or Stanley had never spoken of icebergs while exploring Darkest Africa, they would be dubbed "crazy." Yet conditions are more favorable for the production of icebergs in Africa than in the Arctic Circle, so far as is known. Consider how an iceberg is formed, then see if Africa has not more advantages in the way of forming icebergs than the Arctic Circle. To state again briefly: An iceberg is formed by water running down a stream, where

the mouth freezes early in the fall, and
as the water continues to pass over the
frozen mouth it freezes until spring, when
the warmth from the sun and the water
washing down loosens and plunges it into
the ocean. · In Africa there is the stream
with plenty of rain to furnish water to
freeze, but in the Arctic Circle no rain
or water is found to produce an iceberg.
If there were, the mouth, being warmer
than the interior, would be the last to
freeze, which would stop the flow of water,
the stream being already frozen; and
there being no rain or melted snow, there
would be no water to shove the berg into
the ocean.

So, it will be observed, while it is absolutely impossible for an iceberg to be
formed in Africa, it is not more so than in
the Arctic Circle. Africa lacks only the
cold mouth to the stream, while the Arctic
Circle lacks the cold mouth, the warm interior, and the water to freeze.

Peary has something of intense interest
to say on page 33, where he writes about
the conditions he found on his trip to the

Arctic, and the approach to the Arctic
Ocean through Greenland:

"There, the accumulated snow-precipi-
tation of centuries, in a latitude and altitude where it is practically correct to say
that it never rains, and the snow does not
melt, even in the long summer day, has
gradually filled all the valleys of the interior, until it has leveled them even with
the mountain summits, and, still piling
higher through the centuries, has at last
buried the highest of these mountain summits, hundreds and even thousands of feet
deep in snow and ice.

"The interior of Greenland to-day is
simply an elevated, unbroken plateau of
snow, lifted from five thousand to eight
thousand, and even ten thousand feet
above the level of the sea; a huge, white,
glistening shield twelve hundred miles in
length, and five hundred miles in width,
resting on the supporting mountains.   It
is an Arctic Sahara, in comparison with
which the African Sahara is insignificant.
For on this frozen Sahara of inner Greenland occurs no form of life, animal or

vegetable; no fragment of rock, no grain of sand is visible. The traveler across its frozen wastes, traveling as I have week after week, sees, outside of himself and his own party, but three things in all the world, namely, the infinite expanse of the frozen plain, the infinite dome of the cold, blue sky, and the cold, white sun—nothing but these."

This shows that Greenland is not the country, nor has it the conditions for forming icebergs, as there is no rain, or melted snow; and, so far as I have been able to learn, the discharge from the glaciers is water and not ice. The cold end of the streams or cañons, which could furnish water for icebergs, is to the south, or inland, and the warm end is to the farthest point north. These conditions must be reversed in order to produce an iceberg.

In the following quotation from "The World's Wonders," page 704, a theory is advanced as to how icebergs may be formed:

"Is it not possible that the commonly accepted theory as to the manner in which icebergs are formed is false? If repeated congelation destroys the saline crystallization of sea water, may not a similar chemical decomposition take place under continuous congealment? The rivers of Greenland, to whose debouchment the formation of icebergs is ascribed, are yet to be discovered, though the point of apparent iceberg formation has been visited. It is an open question yet whether these ice mountains are not created under atmospheric influence. If, as seems to be well proved, there is a comparatively warm climate prevailing about the poles, the proximity of excessive cold and warm currents would be productive of the most violent paroxysms of the air, such as cyclones, waterspouts, etc. These might suck up vast quantities of sea water, which would be precipitated again at certain points, like the vapor of the Gulf-Stream, which condenses and falls over England because it there first meets with a counter cold current. If this uplifted water, now vaporized, should strike against the mountain barriers along the Greenland coast it would certainly be precipitated in the form of rain, and, meeting with an intensely cold atmosphere, would congeal as it gradually fell, thus building up great peaks of fresh water ice, just as we see them. This theory might extend further with perfect consistency, to account for icebergs of fresh water by repeated congelations, for it is plausible to assume that there are air strata of hot and cold at altitudes above the poles, passing through which the sea water would alternate from rain to hail, until the chemical change to fresh water is complete. Not infrequently icebergs, or rather, glaciers, form in the interior of Greenland, and always at the feet of mountains or slopes to the sea; after reaching a certain size, gravity causes them to break loose and sweep into the sea, carrying with them great boulders, driftwood, or anything in their path."

When one takes into account the roundabout way in which this writer goes at forming icebergs, my theory of just plain water flowing into the Arctic Ocean, where the mouth freezes, and the balance of the stream keeps open, with water flowing over the frozen mouth, for seven to ten months, will be more successful in producing an iceberg than where dependence is placed upon rain—especially in a country where there is no rain. Remember, Peary says it never rains, and the snow does not melt. In proof of that assertion, he furthermore says the snow is from five to ten thousand feet deep.

Bernacchi mentions huge icebergs traveling northwest at about four knots per hour, coming from the southeast right out of the open sea, on their way north. Could they have left a track, it would have led to the interior of the earth—which is where they had their origin.

Concerning the scarcity of rain and snow in the Arctic regions, which precludes the possibility of furnishing a sufficient quantity of water to produce an iceberg, Nansen says, on page 335, "Why will it not snow? Christmas is near, and what is Christmas without snow, thickly falling snow? We have not had one snowfall all the time we have been drifting."

A SECTION OF THE GREAT ICE BARRIER.

A monster iceberg in the Antarctic Ocean, four hundred miles long, fifty miles wide, grounded in twenty-one hundred feet of water, and extending from one hundred to two hundred feet above the ocean; frozen from fresh water, not attached to land. How did it get there?

When Bernacchi was voyaging in the Antarctic Circle, he wrote:

"During the next two days (11th and 12th) we passed some thousands of icebergs, as many as ninety being counted from the bridge at one time. There was very little variety of form among them, all being very large and bounded by perpendicular cliffs on all sides; they were on an average one hundred and twenty feet in height. Each one of them was a centre of condensation, for over each was a white, vaporous cloud. Could an eye from aloft look down upon the scene, the upper side of the cloud stratum would present somewhat the appearance of an immense cauldron boiling and bubbling and intermixing in the upper air. These icebergs facilitate the formation of clouds and promote precipitation. There was a considerable fall in the specific gravity of the sea, due to the presence of a large quantity of fresh water at the surface, derived from the number of icebergs." (Page 60.)

How does this account accord with your notion of how icebergs are formed in a country where Bernacchi reports less than two inches of rainfall in a whole year, and but small quantities of snow? Where is the water to come from that will produce such great quantities of icebergs averaging a thousand feet in thickness, and many of them several miles long? Those icebergs were on their way north—never to return—yet the ocean will always be filled with them, as others will come from the place whence *they* came. Where is that place? There is no rain or melted snow to furnish the water to freeze into an iceberg. Bergs can come from one place only—the *interior* of the earth.

Bernacchi's speaking of fresh water, in connection with the ice, leads me to believe that that fresh water was held in position just as his ship was—by an unusually strong centre of gravity, it being about the turning point, or half-way round the entrance, to the interior of the earth at the south. My reason for thinking so is, that if it was not an unusually strong centre of gravity, the fresh water would mix with the salt. Gravity draws the heaviest substance strongest. Salt water, being heavier than fresh water, is drawn so firmly that it keeps the two from mixing. This is just what Nansen found in the Arctic,—which he called dead water,—where the fresh water lay on the salt water, and did not mix, but moved with the *Fram*—the bottom of the ship passing down into the salt water was almost like being aground in mud. He could scarcely make any headway, and turned his ship in every direction to free himself of it, but with little success. It was a great relief to find himself free of the dead water, which he had labored to clear his ship of for three days. I know no other reason why fresh and salt water should come together and not mix. If this be the correct explanation, it will account for so much ice being held in large drifts at certain locations, and being shoved along by very heavy winds, or replaced by other large floes which push it on. It will be remembered that Nansen drifted in this ice five months, and only advanced one degree.

On page 263 Bernacchi speaks of the

Great Ice Barrier, and refutes what others have written about it. "It appears as if the ice barrier is nothing more than a huge tongue of ice flowing eastward into the ocean for a distance of perhaps five hundred miles, and possibly not more than fifty miles in width." "The heavy ice-pack met with near this spot tends to prove the existence of a considerable tract of ocean to the south, whose frozen surface breaks up only late in the year, and moves out and around the extremity of the Great Ice Tongue, or Barrier, in the *usual northwesterly* direction. If an extensive land-area were behind, or farther east, such a large mass of sea-ice would be impossible." "Sir James Ross reported the 'appearance of land' to the south of a spot near where we landed on the barrier. We did not, however, sight any, although *we had exceptionally fine, clear weather*."

I *contend* that the *greatest of all icebergs* found in the Antarctic Ocean—called the Great Ice Barrier—is an iceberg, while not formed as most icebergs are,

and not at all like those found in the Arctic Ocean—where they are much shorter,
showing that the streams they come from
flow through a more hilly or mountainous
country than will be found leading to the
opening of the interior of the earth at the
south.   The long icebergs that Bernacchi
speaks of—he calls them "tongues of ice"
—are just the same as this monster, only
smaller.   Writers who claim that the
Great Ice Barrier is a glacier, are surely
in error.   Why should the Great Ice Barrier be the shape of the other ice tongues
found in the Antarctic Ocean?   And how
could a glacier form without land to start
on?   Glaciers are not of that shape.

This berg undoubtedly came from the
interior of the earth.   Why not ascribe a
plain, reasonable construction to the origin
of this great iceberg, in preference to some
absurd theory that cannot be understood?
And if understood, cannot be believed.
Are we still to believe that the earth stands
still, and is solid or flat?   Then it matters but little what the Great Ice Barrier
is called, or how it was formed.

CHAPTER XVII.

THE TIDAL WAVE.

As I contend that many tidal waves are caused by icebergs plunging into the ocean, let us see what grounds there are for that belief. First, something causes the waves: they do not start of their own accord. If an iceberg were to plunge into the ocean, a great commotion would be raised and several large waves would be started. But how far would they run? That would depend upon many different conditions—such as the size of the wave and the force that set it moving. A pebble falling five feet will make but a small ripple, while a rock ten feet in diameter, falling one hundred feet, will make a mighty wave. Then, if no obstructions be met, and the wind be favorable, that wave would go a long way. According to Wells's "Natural Philosophy," it might get larger instead of smaller. "This wave," says he, "propagates itself

into the unmoved space adjoining, continually enlarging as it goes, and forming a
series of undulations." Again: "When
two systems of waves, coming from different centres, meet, some curious effects are
produced. If like phases in both systems
coincide, or if the crest of one system coin-
cides with the crest of the other, the new
wave will be equal to the sum of the two
originals."

A wave is a form, not a thing; the form
advances, but not the substance of the
wave. Two icebergs might frequently
plunge in from different directions, and
send forth just such conditions as Wells
writes about. Or the one plunging in first
might be farther away, and as waves move
comparatively slowly, they might frequently meet at some common centre, and
be increased in size and force, as he
suggests.

Could anything else produce so large
a wave? If not, why should we not give
the greatest cause credit for the greatest
effect? The wonderful ice-pressure can
be produced from different causes: winds,

tides, currents, and tidal waves. The tidal wave, however, makes it puzzling; for it comes when there is no wind or current, and if the tidal-wave theory were excluded it certainly would be a hard proposition to answer. If the pressure occurred only when the current changed, or the wind blew, or the tides set in or out, the question of ice-pressure would never have been wondered at. In the absence of those natural causes, it was the pressure that set people thinking and wondering how such things could be. Any close observer who reads the reports of the different explorers will have noticed how mysterious are many things in the Arctic regions. If a musk-ox were found growing fast to a rock, I doubt whether such an occurrence would excite more wonder than many things in that wonderful country, hitherto unexplained. One meets, no doubt, with many radical changes and puzzling situations—such as a change from the interior of the earth to the exterior would necessarily produce; and when one takes into account that no one knew that the earth was hollow, and supposed that whatever brought about those strange conditions was to be accounted for in a few hundred miles' journey straight north to the pole, it is not to be wondered at that people called it "the mysterious land," especially when one saw the surface of the ice, water, and land reflected in the sky and could not see a great fire.   If they *did* see it, they called it something else—the aurora, a mock sun, a double moon, or some other wonderful phenomenon; yet nothing is mysterious when fully understood.

The perplexing situations met with in the Arctic Circle, the grand scenes of every kind, and the things difficult to understand, remind one of the man reading the dictionary: the words were fine, but he couldn't make much of the story.

It is so with the explorers: everything is grand; the ice roars, and crushes when everything is calm; the heavens are lighted up most beautifully when there is no storm; the winds blow terribly out of the clear sky: none of these things can be understood.

Nansen's second volume, page 29, of "Farthest North" describes what that famous explorer experienced from ice-pressure—caused, doubtless, by tidal waves: "To-day, about 12.30 p. m., the *Fram* received another violent shock, even stronger than that we had experienced during the night. There was another shake a little later. I suppose there has been a pressure aft, but could hear nothing for the storm. It is odd about this pressure; one would think that the wind was the primary cause; but it recurs pretty regularly, notwithstanding the fact that the spring tide has not yet set in; indeed, when it commenced a few days ago, it was almost a neap tide. In addition to the pressure of yesterday and last night, we had pressure on Thursday morning, at half-past nine, and again at half-past eleven. It was so strong that Peter, who was at the sounding-hole, jumped up repeatedly, thinking that the ice would burst underneath him. It is very singular, we have been quiet for so long now that we feel almost nervous when the *Fram* receives these shocks;

everything seems to tremble as if in a violent earthquake."

Nansen's remarks about the tide having nothing to do with ice-pressure, must be accounted for in some other way. That *other* way is a tidal wave.

In the same volume, farther on, he says: "The ice-pressure was not noticeable after 1 o'clock on Friday night until it suddenly recommenced last night. First I heard a rumbling outside, and some snow fell down from the rigging upon the tent-roof as I sat reading; I thought it sounded like packing in the ice, and just then the *Fram* received a violent shock, such as she had not received last winter. I was rocked backward and forward on the chest on which I was sitting. Finding that the trembling and rumbling continued, I went out. There was a loud roar of ice, packing to the west and northwest, which continued uniformly for a couple of hours or so. * * * Just after I had come on board again, shortly before noon, the ice suddenly began to press on again. I went out to have a look; it was again in the

lane on the port side; there was a strong
pressure, and the ridge was gradually approaching. A little later on Sverdrup
went up on deck, but soon after came below and told us that the ridge was quickly
bearing down on us."

When speaking of ice-pressure, nearly
all explorers speak of great ridges. Melville calls it a "frozen wave." Bernacchi
says the ice was lifted seventy, eighty, and
ninety feet. Nansen termed it a ridge;
and all agree that they look like great
ridges, or waves, that can be heard for
miles in the distance before they reach the
ship, and for a long time after they have
passed. If the descriptions given by the
several explorers do not correctly repre-
sent a set of great waves, I do not know
how to describe them.

Melville describes, in expressive manner,
a scene in which ice-pressure played a part
during his sojourn in the Arctic regions.
"It was in one of these oppressive inter-
vals succeeding a gale," says he, "when the
roar and crash of the distant masses could
be distinctly heard, that the floe in which

the *Jeannette* was imbedded began splitting in all directions. The placid and almost level surface of ice suddenly heaved and swelled into great hills, buzzing and wheezing dolefully. Giant blocks pitched and rolled as though controlled by invisible hands, and the vast compressing bodies shrieked a shrill and horrible song that curdled the blood. On came the frozen waves, nearer and nearer. Seams ran and rattled across them with a thundering boom, while silent and awe-struck we watched their terrible progress." (Page 12.)

The reader will notice that these weird doings occurred after a storm; and during it the ice, as a whole, moved along with but slight disturbance. The swell that comes after a storm has no connection with it. If a storm raises no swell after raging continuously for ten to twenty-four hours, it would take a great deal to make me believe that after it had subsided it had anything to do with the swell that came later. Melville's description, just cited, proves to my mind that the whole affair arose from a series of tidal waves. The later storm had nothing to do with what he calls "frozen waves." They were caused by some tremendous agency, and I can conceive of nothing more powerful than the plunging of an iceberg into the ocean. Anyone knows that when an iceberg plunges into the sea it causes the greatest commotion imaginable, and as the tremendous swells referred to are constantly experienced, why should not the icebergs produce them? If, at a certain point on a river, laborers are engaged in rolling saw logs into the water from a high bank,—causing heavy swells to wash up against the opposite shore,—would it be a stretch of the imagination to say—if asked what caused the swells—that men were rolling logs into the water on the other side? On the contrary, it would be rather stupid on the part of the questioner if he knew what was being done. We know that icebergs plunge into the ocean, and we ought to know that when this happens they make the largest possible wave. As soon as anyone can show what becomes of those waves and that they are *not* the waves that tumble and crush the ice so terribly—and, at the same time, tell where those waves come from that do the damage—it will then be time to reconsider this statement; but not till then. Icebergs are very numerous; and so are those waves. Melville says, "one body of ice set in motion crowds on ice not in motion." That is true, but the wind does not need to' stop to bring about that condition of things.

Nansen's accounts of this subject are most appropriate. On page 278 of Volume I, he says: "We had kept company quite long enough with the old—now broken-up—floe, so worked ourselves a little way astern after dinner, as the ice was beginning to draw together.

"Towards evening the pressure began again in earnest, and was especially bad around the remains of our floe, so that I believe we may congratulate ourselves on having left it. It is evident that the pressure here stands in connection with—is perhaps caused by—the tidal wave. It occurs with the greatest regularity. The ice slackens twice and packs twice in twenty-four hours. The pressure has happened about 4, 5, and 6 o'clock in the morning, and almost exactly the same hour in the afternoon, and in between we have always lain for some part of the time in open water. The very great pressure just now is probably due to the spring tide; we had new moon on the 9th, which was the first day of the pressure. Then it was just after mid-day when we noticed it, but it has been later every day, and now it is at 8 p. m."

Farther on, in the same volume, we read: "For when the packing begins in earnest it seems as though there could be no spot on the earth's surface left unshaken. First you hear a sound like the thundering rumbling of an earthquake far away on the great waste; then you hear it in several places, always coming nearer and nearer. The silent ice world re-echoes with thunders; Nature's giants are awakening to the battle. The ice cracks on every side of you, and begins to pile itself up; and all of a sudden you, too, find yourself in the midst of the struggle. There are howlings and thunderings round you; you feel the ice tremble, and hear it rumbling under your feet; there is no peace anywhere. In the semi-darkness you can see it piling and tossing itself up into high ridges nearer and nearer you —floes ten, twelve, fifteen feet thick, broken, and flung on the top of each other as if they were feather-weights. They are quite near you now, and you jump away to save your life. But the ice splits in front of you, a black gulf opens, and water streams up. You turn in another direction, but there through the dark you can just see a new ridge of moving ice-blocks coming towards you. You try another direction, but there it is the same. All around there is thundering and roaring, as of some enormous waterfall, with explosions like cannon salvoes. Still nearer you it comes. The floe you are standing on gets smaller and smaller; water pours over it; there can be no escape except by scrambling over the rolling ice-blocks to get to the other side of the pack.

But now the disturbance begins to calm
down.   The noise passes on, and is lost
by degrees in the distance."

On page 383 Nansen begins other descriptions that are worth reproducing:

"Most violent pressures are beginning
again.   I must go on deck and look at it.
The loud roar. meets one as one opens the
door.   It is coming from the bow now,
as well as from the stern.   It is clear that
the pressure ridges are being thrown up
in both openings, so if they reach us we
shall be taken by both ends and lifted
lightly and gently out of the water.   There
is pressure near us on all sides.   Creaking
has begun in the old hummock on the port
quarter; it is getting louder, and, so far
as I can see, the hummock is slowly rising.
A lane has opened right across the large
floe on the port side; you can see the water,
dark as it is.   Now both pressure and
noise get worse and worse; the ship shakes
and I feel as if I myself were being gently
lifted with the stern rail, where I stand
gazing out at the welter of ice masses that
resemble giant snakes writhing and twist-

ing their great bodies out there under the quiet, starry sky, whose peace is only broken by one aurora serpent waving and flickering restlessly in the northeast.

"Saturday, January 27.—It is remarkable that we should have this strong pressure just now, with the moon in its last quarter and neap tide. This does not agree with our previous experiences; no more does the fact that the pressure the day before yesterday was from 12 a. m. to about 2 p. m., and then again at 2 a. m., and now we have had it from 7.30 to 10.30 p. m. Can land have something to do with it here, after all? The temperature to-day is 42 deg. Fahr. below zero (—41.4 deg.), but there is no wind, and we have not had such pleasant weather for walking for a long time; it feels almost mild here when the air is still.

"No, that was not the end of the pressure. When I was on deck, at a quarter to 12, roaring and trembling began in the ice forward on the port side; then suddenly came one loud boom after another, sounding out in the distance, and the ship gave a start; there was again a little pressure, and after that quietness. Strange to say, there has been no pressure since 12 o'clock last night; the ice seems perfectly quiet. The pressure ridge astern showed what violent packing yesterday's was; in one place its height was eighteen to nineteen feet above the surface of the water; floe-ice eight feet thick was broken, pressed up in square blocks, and crushed to pieces. At one point a huge monolith of such floe-ice rose high into the air. Beyond this pressure wall there was no great disturbance to be detected. There had been a little packing here and there, and the floe to port had four or five large cracks across it, which no doubt accounted for the explosion I heard last night. The ice to starboard was also cracked in several places. The pressure had evidently come from the North or N. N. E. The ridge behind us is one of the highest I have ever seen yet. I believe that if the *Fram* had been lying there she would have been lifted right out of the water. I walked for some distance in a northeasterly direction, but saw no signs of pressure there. When the ice has been set adrift in a certain direction by the wind blowing that way for some time, it gradually in process of drifting becomes more compressed, and when the wind dies away a reaction in the opposite direction takes place. Such a reaction must, I believe, have been the cause of Saturday's pressure, which stopped entirely as suddenly as it began. Since then there has not been the slightest appearance of movement in the ice. Probably the pressure indicates the time when the drift turned."

Concerning ice - pressure, Bernacchi, writing of his voyage in the Antarctic, on page 120, vividly conveys to the reader a picture of what he saw. "A deep sonorous roar was audible like the din of a battle; a battle indeed! A great battle of Nature was raging. We rushed down towards the shore from whence the noise came, and on reaching it a sight met our eyes which baffles description; a scene absolutely frightful in its grandeur. A moving mountain of ice had risen up; a sudden and terrible pressure had set in, was piling the ice on the shore. It extended for about eight hundred yards, and was on an average sixty feet high; the mass was moving the whole time and advancing upon the land. The grandeur of the spectacle was immense. There is nothing comparable to it, and words can in no degree convey an idea of the majesty of the scene.

"Huge blocks of ice, thousands and thousands of tons in weight, were lifted up seventy, eighty, and ninety feet with irresistible force to the top of the mount. They would totter for a few seconds, and then come crashing down with a reverberating roar; at times great yawning gaps would appear in the mount, and the whole side would bulge out until with a fearful crash it would burst, and great blocks of ice fly into the air like so many straws."

This great disturbance lasted a little more than an hour. There is no account of any storm or wind, so its cause must be accounted for in some other way. We will call it a set of mammoth waves started by the plunging of an iceberg into the ocean.

The indefatigable Peary, on page 30, describes the effect of ice-pressure: "One forenoon the barometer dropped rapidly, and in the afternoon the snow ceased, the clouds lifted, and a tremendous swell came rolling in from the southeast. Not a breath of wind disturbed the surface as the long, lazy swells, smoothed by the pressure of the ice through which they passed, came slipping noiselessly in, lifting and dropping the huge bergs as if they were but corks."

Can anyone read the description of ice-pressure, as given here, and say it was not a set of tidal waves, or large waves, set in motion by some powerful influence? What is more irresistible than an immense iceberg plunging into the ocean—one, for instance, a mile long, a thousand feet thick, and half a mile wide, under fair speed when it strikes the ocean? Such a berg would go to the bottom unless there was a depth of many thousand feet. Imagine, if possible, the commotion produced.

CHAPTER XVIII.

CLOUDS, FOGS, AND VAPORS.

The fog, clouds, vapor, and peculiar kind of snow met with at the poles ought to set one to thinking what produces them. There are too many peculiar conditions to come from no particular cause, and all just alike at the North and South poles. Take Africa and Norway, regions which are not at all alike in anything—the game, the vegetation, the people, the climates are as different as the pies a man's wife makes from those his mother used to make. Yet if one travels in the opposite direction, till one reaches the Arctic and Antarctic circles, all become as like as one is to himself.

The earth being hollow, the atmosphere in passing out, either north or south, would affect the country it passes into in the same manner. That is why one finds so many things in common in both polar regions: vapors, snows, auroras, winds, and falling meteors, each locality filled

with fowl, warmer, and open water. The
following extracts, with comments thereon, will throw some light on this interesting subject. Peary says: "On the
ice-cap a fresh breeze was blowing, and
though the sun was shining brightly, and
there was blue sky overhead, all the upper part of McCormick Bay was hidden
by lead-colored cumulus clouds, and Ingle-
field Gulf lay invisible behind a dazzling
white mist." (Page 232.)

Nothing appears to be so common in the
Far Northern regions as those low, dark
cumulus clouds, that are frequently seen
rising on the horizon, or, as it is frequently expressed, from the ocean, while
the sky is perfectly clear and the sun shining brightly. Nothing but warmer air
from the interior of the earth could produce such clouds. This could not, or
would not, be the case if the earth were
solid: there is no reason why it should be
warmer near the poles.

The earth obtains its heat from the sun;
and yet when one is where the sun's
rays do not strike the earth for months

at a time, it is found that the north winds are warmer than the south winds. This fact ought to suggest that that wind must come from some place other than the North Pole. The interior of the earth is the only place from which warm winds could come in the winter.

The same explorer says on pages 314 and 315: "Another discouraging day within sight of the baleful shores of this Arctic Sahara, but we are on the heights once more—for good, I hope, and, I also trust, free from further obstacles. If there is any truth in the superstition of the evil eye, the coast of this Inland Ice surely has evil eyes. Just as long as the black cliffs peer up at us over the round of the ice-cap, just so long are we beset with crevasses, slippery ice, hummocks, howling wind storms, furious drifts, and fogs."

This term "evil eye" seems to apply to conditions that are usually found on reaching the extreme north, as Peary speaks of being beset with crevasses, slippery ice, hummocks, howling winds, furious drifts, and fogs. Those are just the conditions one would meet with if the earth were hollow. Note that Peary says the black cliffs peer up *over* the ice-cap. In making the turn when the earth curves, one cliff or projection would follow like the spokes to the wheel of a wagon—one comes up as one goes under. While the earth's curve is not so short as one might imagine, yet it is short enough to make things appear strange to persons looking for level country to the pole. The clouds, mists, slippery ice, etc., are just what one would meet in summer at the entrance to the interior of the earth; yet if the earth is solid there is no reason why they should be met.

Bernacchi gives descriptions of weather conditions in the southern polar regions that have a bearing on this subject. On page 264 he says: "A dense mist lay over the water, which made it impossible to see any farther than the length of the ship. The mist or vapor was in a state of congelation, so that the whole ship was covered in frost rime. This mist was no more than fifty feet high, and in the crow's-nest it was a gloriously fine day, not a cloud being visible in the sky, and the sun shining brightly over the barrier (ice barrier). On deck it was too thick to see anything." Page 266, he says: "The fog was so dense that we were compelled to stop and lay-to for some time. During the night the temperature sank to 3° 8 F. When the wind changed to E. and N. E., it immediately rose to + 17° F."

CHAPTER XIX.

ARCTIC AND ANTARCTIC WINDS.

This book has but one purpose—to prove that the earth is hollow. Therefore, instead of trying to make an entertaining argument, I prefer making a plain, convincing one. For that reason, some may think I have spent too much time on certain phases of my argument, yet I believe I will be able to convince the reader in every point I make. If I convince him in one case, the rest need no argument. Let us take up the question of the wind, a subject that has received the best thoughts of our great scientific men. These scientists cannot agree upon what makes the wind act so strangely at the poles. Peary says that at the North Pole "it is invariably radial from the centre outward, perpendicular, so steady is this wind and so closely does it adhere to the perpendicularity."

How does the Antarctic explorer find

the wind? If the earth be hollow, as the wind passes through the earth it would operate about the same at either entrance —under similar conditions. For instance, a great volcanic explosion at the southern end would send forth a great force of warm, dry air, which would blow out radially and upward, and spread in all directions. This is done so universally that certain writers have termed it an anti-cyclone. It must, of course, have a name, and why not call it anti-cyclone, although Granny Cyclone would be more appropriate. Call it what you please, it is the wind passing out from the interior of the earth, and when released, it spreads in every direction. The descriptions given by Peary of the Arctic winds and by Bernacchi of the Antarctic, are alike.

Bernacchi says on page 112: "On the morning of May 4th a gale burst upon us with great fury and with little warning; ten minutes before its first burst it blew in whirlwinds, then came a great rush, bringing with it tons of drifting snow. It was the strongest gale we had as yet experi-

THE EMPEROR PENGUIN.

Found at the farthest point reached in the Antarctic
Circle. It must migrate for food in winter, but it cannot fly. If the earth is not hollow, where does this bird
go when the ice prevents it from swimming?

enced, and it blew with fearful potency all day. Just previous to the first outburst the barometer had commenced to fall and reached its minimum reading, 28.227 inches, just before the wind dropped, at 9 p. m. These winds, always from the same direction, are a remarkable feature in the meteorology of the Antarctic. Some meteorologists have held that a vast cyclonic system and low-pressure area continues south as far as the pole, the more southerly parts being traversed by secondary cyclones; others contend that the extreme south-polar area is occupied by a vast anticyclone, out of which winds blow toward the girdle of low pressure.

"The prevailing east-southeast and southeast winds at Cape Adare (lat. 71 deg. 18 min.), which is within the area of abnormally low pressure, tend to prove the existence of a great anti-cyclone stretching over the polar area, which in its turn necessarily implies the existence of upper currents from the north, blowing towards and in upon the polar regions to make good the drain caused by the surface outblowing southeasterly winds."

Bernacchi, page 129, after giving details of a great storm, says: "About this time a very fine specimen of an Emperor penguin was caught out on the ice-pack; a big, sad, solitary bird, over four feet high. The presence of these birds so far south late in the year proves that they do not migrate far north during the Antarctic winter."

This was when the temperature registered 2 deg. below zero. The penguin is a flightless bird and must seek its food in open water. If the earth be not hollow, where does this bird migrate to in winter for food? These birds are found at the farthest point south.

I will now give you a description of an anti-cyclone, written by Bernacchi, that you may see if there be any difference between it and Perry's Arctic wind. To account for this surface-wind blowing outward, it is said that it must blow down from the north from an upper current. If so, one might, naturally, ask, why would it be warmer, dryer, and always from the same direction?

No, it does not come from above; it comes from the interior of the earth, which accounts for its being warmer, dryer, and always from the same direction, except on days when the air is sucked into the interior of the earth. The following is what Bernacchi says about anti-cyclones:

"An anti-cyclone is a portion of the atmosphere in which the pressure is highest at the centre, and diminishes nearly uniformly in all directions, and the winds blow spirally outward. A cyclone is just the reverse, and has the lowest pressure at the centre, and the winds blow in towards this centre of low pressure in a spiral curve.

"The frequency and force of these gales, and the persistency with which they blew—always from the same direction, east-southeast,—the invariably high rise in temperature, and the sudden fall and rise of the barometer, the dryness of the winds —the relative humidity—generally be-

tween fifty and sixty per cent.—and the
motion of the upper clouds from the northwest, point to the fact that the South Pole
is covered by what may be regarded practically as a great permanent anti-cyclone
more extensive in the winter months than
in the summer. Nothing more appalling
than these frightful winds, accompanied
by tons of drift snow from the mountains
above, can be imagined." (Page 115.)

On page 295 Bernacchi gives considerable space to the strange phenomena of
the wind at Cape Adare, where he spent
nearly two years. He also quotes Sir
John Murray, of the *Challenger,* and
others, as meeting the same experience.
If the earth be hollow, this matter of the
wind blowing spirally outward is all right,
as it could not blow any other way. If the
earth be solid, there is no telling why the
wind blows as it does, and consequently
the mystery must remain a mystery. Bernacchi and Sir John Murray mention the
precipitation occurring on the outflowing
winds. One says it was slight, the other
says it was less than two inches in nearly

a year.   These are statements worth re-
membering.   If there is no rain, and the
snow is so slight in amount that it cannot be measured, where does the water
come from that produces the vast number
of icebergs in the Antarctic region?

"The mean temperature of the air for
the eleven months was 5.2 deg. Fahr.;
the amount this E. S. E. wind raises the
mean temperature is 8.8 deg. Fahr.   This
power of raising the temperature is more
conspicuous in the winter time than in
summer.

"Thus the mean temperature for the
month of July is — 9°, while the mean
temperature of the E. S. E. winds for
that month is + 7.6°, a difference of 16.6°
Fahr.   Such a contrast is very striking."
(Page 304.)

The power that this wind has in raising the temperature is perhaps better
shown in the table of single storms,
printed in Bernacchi's work.

On the meteorological conditions, Bernacchi says: "A mere glance at the Cape
Adare wind-roses shows the prevailing

winds from E. S. E. and S. E. *in a very marked degree*. These winds were the most remarkable feature observed in the *meteorological* conditions of Victoria Land. Their frequency and force, the *persistency with which they blew from the same direction,* the invariably *high rise in the temperature,* their dryness, the motion of the upper clouds from the N. W., and, finally, the gradual rise in the mean height of the barometer to the south of about Latitude 73 S. seem to indicate that the Antarctic lands are covered by what may be regarded, practically, as a great permanent anti-cyclone, with a higher pressure than prevails over the open ocean to the northwards.

"While this anti-cyclonic region may not be characterized by an absolutely high pressure at all seasons, it must be high relatively to the very low pressure which prevails to the northwards.

"Sir John Murray, of the *Challenger* expedition, was one of the first to advance the theory of a vast anti-cyclone covering the South Pole, and, on the whole, the observations made at Cape Adare, which is almost at the centre of the area of lowest mean pressure, appear to bear out his views.

"It is, however, impossible to arrive at anything definite respecting the atmospheric circulation over the Antarctic regions from observations taken at one station only."—Bernacchi, pages 295 and 296.

"Sir John Murray has said that we might expect the southerly, outflowing winds which accompany this anti-cyclone to be dry winds, and attended by a small precipitation. At Cape Adare, the belt of excessive precipitation has been passed; the total amount of precipitation registered during the year being under two inches, and of this the greater part fell in the summer or autumn months, when the ocean to the north was practically free of ice, and the amount of evaporation from its surface at its maximum. During the winter months, however, precipitation generally took place from a practically clear, blue sky, in the form of very minute, hard ice-crystals, and in such small quantities as to defy measurement by means of an ordinary snow-gauge."

Peary says, on pages 74 and 75: "The regularity of the winds of the 'Great Ice' of Greenland, as I have found them during an actual sojourn of over seven months upon the 'Great Ice,' and visits to it of greater or less duration in every month of the year, is phenomenal. Except during atmospheric disturbances of unusual magnitude, which cause storms to sweep across the country regardless of ordinary rules, the direction of the wind of the 'Great Ice' of Greenland is invariably radial from the centre outward, perpendicular to the nearest part of the coastland ribbon. So steady is this wind, and so closely does it adhere to this perpendicularity, that I can liken it only to the flow of a sheet of water descending the slopes of the 'Great Ice' from the central interior dome to the coast."

If the earth be hollow, the wind would pass from the interior of the earth, just as has been described many times, blowing strongly and steadily. At other times heavy gusts, as nearly as possible like the explosions of a mammoth air-gun, rush out, as described above.

Nansen, on page 373 (Volume I), also speaks of the temperature rising under the influence of northerly winds. "Thursday, January 18th.—The wind that began yesterday has gone on blowing all to-day with a velocity of sixteen to nineteen feet per second, from S.S.E., S.E. and E.S.E. It has no doubt helped us on a good way north; but it seems to be going down; now, about midnight, it has sunk to four metres; and the barometer, which has been rising all the time, has suddenly begun to fall; let us hope that it is not a cyclone passing over us, bringing northerly wind. It is curious that there is almost always a rise of the thermometer with these strong winds; to-day it rose to 13 deg., Fahr., below zero (— 25 deg. C.). A south wind of less velocity generally lowers the temperature, and a moderate north wind raises it."

Farther on he says: "It is curious that

now the northerly winds bring cold and the southerly warmth. Earlier in the winter it was just the opposite.

"It seems strange to me that there is so much northwest wind, and hardly any from the northeast; though the latter is what the rotation of the earth would lead one to expect. As a matter of fact, the wind merely shifts between northwest and southeast, instead of between southwest and northeast, as it *ought* to do. Unless there is land, I am at a loss to find a satisfactory explanation, at all events, of this northwest direction."

What Nansen says about the change of the wind since winter began, is important, and is another of the strong proofs that the earth is hollow, and that the atmosphere in the interior of the earth is of a more even temperature than on the exterior.

It would also be warmer in winter and colder in summer, which all explorers have found to be the case.

CHAPTER XX.

THE CENTRE OF GRAVITY.

To many, the question of gravity seems a great argument against the theory that the earth is hollow. This undoubtedly arises from the fact that gravity is supposed to be something located in the centre of the earth, drawing everything in that direction, or to the centre. Philosophy teaches that the greater attracts the lesser. If the earth is hollow, and the walls are, say, a thousand miles thick, why should not the centre of the walls be the centre of attraction, as well as of the earth, if solid? If gravity is something that repels ether, or air, above the earth, then it would make no difference whether the earth were concave or convex.

Again: if the centre of the walls of the earth is the centre of gravity, then the greatest attraction would be at the poles, where it is found to be. Nansen's description of the dead water, it will be re-

membered, is: "We could hardly get on
at all, for the dead water, and we swept
the whole sea along with us. It is a peculiar phenomenon—this dead water. We
had at present a better opportunity of
studying it than we desired. It occurs
where a surface layer of fresh water rests
upon the salt water of the sea, and this
fresh water is carried along with the ship,
gliding on the heavier sea water beneath,
as if on a fixed foundation."

The centre of gravity seems strongest
here, and was probably about midway
round the curve on Nansen's way to the
interior of the earth. If this be true, it is
in accordance with the wisdom of the
Creator: the greatest attraction where it
is most needed. The laws of the universe
are inevitable; when they seem otherwise
we do not understand them.

The question of gravity is most puzzling, and, so far as I know, not understood. I desire to show that, be the earth
hollow or solid, gravity is not in any way
affected. If gravity is something that
acts as a magnet, and draws everything to

the centre, the walls of the earth would then be the magnet. On the other hand, if gravity is something *above* the earth that repels—air or ether—then the earth's shape would in nowise affect it. I believe it will be found that gravity is strongest at the turning point entering the interior of the earth, and objects will weigh more at that point than near the equator or in the interior of the earth. Every substance will then appear lighter or weigh less in the interior of the earth, for the reason that the laws of the universe are so perfect that nothing is wasted, and a substance requires less force to hold it to the inside of a hollow ball in motion than to hold it to the outside.

CHAPTER XXI.

CANNOT REACH THE POLES.

That the earth is hollow is proved by the fact that no one can get to the poles. In recent years all explorers have made practically the same progress—from 80 to 84 deg. latitude—and all agree that they find it warmer, and with an open sea. The difference of a few degrees is owing to the longitude as well as latitude when taking observations. The land is not necessarily the farthest north. The curve leading to the interior of the earth may be land or water, just as it happens, and he that passes to the farthest point of the circle when the observation is taken, will show the farthest point north. But if he continues straight on he will soon be losing ground, or getting farther from the supposed pole, and eventually be going south and not know it, as the compass could not then be depended upon. There must be some good reason

why all have been obliged to turn back
after reaching latitude 80 deg. to 84 deg.
They have passed through a much colder

A bird's-eye view of the opening to the interior of the
earth.

climate, where there were more ice, less
open water, and no game or signs of life;
yet at this point all failed.   It is like looking into the water and seeing the reflec-

tion of the moon, then getting into a boat and trying to get it. The moon always keeps some distance away; and so it is with the PHANTOM OF THE POLES.

I have quoted from nearly all the explorers, for the purpose of showing that, at the farthest point reached, either north or south, they found it warmer, with open water and plenty of game. Their remarks also prove, beyond a doubt, that what I claim is true—that the Arctic and Antarctic oceans are bodies of open water, abounding with game of all kinds, and much warmer than farther inland. If that is true, then why have the poles not been reached? The poles are but phantoms—the earth is hollow, or all principle of reasoning must fail.

CHAPTER XXII.

WHAT IS IN THE INTERIOR OF THE EARTH?

I have been asked what I expect to find in the interior of the earth. That, of course, is speculative, based on the little evidence found on earth. It is not like the question, "Is the earth hollow?" We know that it is, but do not know what will be found in its interior. It is like seeing an island afar off: we know there is land, but do not know what it is like till we get there. So many circumstances show the earth is hollow that the fact cannot be questioned; but its contents are not so easily determined till we look inside. From what I am able to gather, and from analysis, game of all kinds—tropical and arctic—will be found there; for both warm and cold climates must be in the interior—warm inland and cold near the poles. Sea monsters, and possibly the much-talked-of sea serpent, may also be found, and vast territories of arable land for farming purposes. This theory is based upon the great quantities of pollen that finds its way to the exterior of the earth, and falls with the snow in such great quantities that it colors it, and thus produces the colored snow of the Arctic Circle. This would require millions of acres of land to grow. Minerals may be found in great quantities, and gems of all kinds. The earth contains minerals and gems, and they are as likely to be in the interior of the earth as on the exterior. ·We may succeed, too, in finding large quantities of radium, which would be used to relieve the darkness if it should be unusually dark. I do not think this will be the case, however, as there are two summers of four months' duration and two winters of two months', giving the interior eight months of summer and four months of winter in each of our years on earth. In other words, the years in the interior of the earth are but six months long, and every other year the summer becomes a little longer and the winter a little shorter. The two just make up the six months.

Why? Because the opening into the interior of the earth at the south, or Antarctic, is fifteen hundred miles in diameter, or forty-five hundred miles in circumference; while the opening into the interior of the earth at the north, or Arctic, is only one thousand miles in diameter, or three thousand miles in circumference. The sun would begin to shine in the interior of the earth from the south several days earlier than at the north, simply because the opening is five hundred miles wider; for the same reason it would disappear later. That would make the summer—supplied with light and heat from the Antarctic—longer, and the winter shorter than the summer which derived its heat and light from the north, as the opening to the interior of the earth is five hundred miles less in diameter than the opening to the south. The sun consequently would appear later, and disappear earlier, making shorter the summers deriving their heat and light from the north, and the winters longer. This seems to me reasonable and correct.

The dimensions of the openings at the poles are arrived at in this way: The magnetic poles, both north and south, have been reached, one five hundred miles from the supposed pole, and the other seven hundred and fifty miles, making one thousand and one thousand five hundred miles to the poles, as only one side is estimated. Timber of good size will be found, as shown by driftwood on the shores of the fiords, islands, and inlets of the Arctic. I also believe that the interior of the earth will be found inhabited. The race or races may be varied, but some at least will be of the Eskimo race, who have found their way in from the exterior. Camping places have been discovered, and relics that did not belong to the present Innuits; nor did the latter know for what purposes certain articles were used. The climate will be much more even than on earth, as shown by the winds coming from the interior, which are much warmer in winter and much cooler in summer than on earth. It is about such a climate as San Francisco, I should judge, where one has to stop to think whether it is June or January.

I have been asked about the risk and manner of getting there. Some risks are to be taken, of course; and dangers are to be guarded against. For instance, an iceberg plunging into the ocean would swamp a ship, if near. This can be guarded against, however, by sending out scouts, or keeping away from the shore. To me it does not seem especially dangerous.

In going into the earth's interior special care should be taken to guard against all conceivable accidents; as no pilot can be had for the first trip to steer clear of breakers, etc. A ship should be well supplied with very fast auxiliary boats and powerful searchlights, in order that the ship have the best and safest course. Some plan should be found by which to steer a boat without a compass in foggy weather, which will have to be done when passing through and round the turn into the interior of the earth. Stations should be placed within a few miles of each other, supplied with wireless telegraphy instruments, manned by able operators, so that hourly communications can be had when passing unusually dangerous points,—should any be found.

I have a plan for the strengthening of a ship, which seems a good one; but as I am not a shipbuilder there may be objections to it. A strong ship should be built in the usual way, then have from three to five large and strong timbers—not too heavy (Georgia pine)—placed across the ship,—not fastened to her, but held in position, so that in rough weather they could not move out of place. Each timber should be in two pieces, and put together by large adjustable screws, that when in the vicinity of bergs they could be extended several feet over the edge of the ship. When a berg approached the ship and she was crowded against another berg, the timbers would be pressed endwise and thus protect her from being crushed, as a piece of timber two feet square would resist a greater pressure when pressed endwise than any ship's hull could be made to stand.   Take a small lead pencil, and note its resistance when pressed endwise.   The object of not having the timbers fastened to the ship, is to keep them from straining or harming her.

IN CONCLUSION.

The earth is either hollow or it is not. What proof have we concerning the latter? Not one iota, positive or circumstantial. On the contrary, everything points to its being hollow. If it be so, and there are burning volcanoes in the interior, would you not see great lights reflected on the icebergs and the clouds just as any other great fires reflect the light? Would not great clouds of smoke and dust be seen?—the same as from any other burning volcano? That is what all the explorers have witnessed—low, dark clouds rising out of the ocean, or at the edge of the ice. Nansen says: "Let us go home; what have we here to stay for? Nothing but dust, dust, dust." Where could such dust come from—so bad that it was one of the great annoyances in the heart of the Arctic Ocean—if it did not come from an exploding, burning volcano? If the earth be hollow, would it not be warmer in winter and cooler in summer?

Arctic explorers say that a north wind

in winter raises the temperature, while a south wind lowers it. As an opposite fact, in summer a south wind raises the temperature and a north wind lowers it. This is just what would occur if the winds came from the interior of the earth. Again: if the earth be hollow, it could not be round, inasmuch as the opening would take from its roundness in proportion to the size of the opening. All now agree that the earth is flattened at the poles. Also, it is warmer the farther one goes north or south. Why is this the case?

There is but one answer, and that is that the earth is hollow, and is warmer in the interior than on the exterior. As the wind passes out in the winter it warms the atmosphere. If the earth be solid, neither science nor reason furnishes any rational theory why it should be warmer as one passes north. Every known theory is against such a conclusion. As soon as you adopt the belief that the earth is hollow, perplexing questions will be easily solved, the mind will be satisfied, and the triumph of sensible reasoning will come as a delight never to be forgotten.

CPSIA information can be obtained at www.ICGtesting.com
Printed in the USA
BVOW08*0022040116

431631BV00005B/122/P

9 781165 015634